Building Exceptional Sites
with WordPress & Thesis

by
Peter MacIntyre

A™ a php[architect] guide

Building Exceptional Sites with WordPress & Thesis

First Edition: May 2016
ISBN - Print: 978-1-940111-31-5
ISBN - PDF: 978-1-940111-32-2
ISBN - ePub: 978-1-940111-33-9
ISBN - Mobi: 978-1-940111-34-6
ISBN - Safari: 978-1-940111-35-3
Produced & Printed in the United States

Disclaimer

Written by
Peter MacIntyre

Published by
musketeers.me, LLC.
201 Adams Ave.
Alexandria, VA 22301
USA

240-348-5PHP (240-348-5747)

info@phparch.com
www.phparch.com

Editor-in-Chief
Oscar Merida

Managing Editor
Eli White

Technical Reviewer
Oscar Merida

Copy Editor
Kara Ferguson

Layout and Design
Kevin Bruce

Table of Contents

Dedication   VII

Acknowledgments   IX

Foreword   XI

Chapter 1.   Requirements   1

    HTML & CSS   1
    Environments   1
    WordPress Install   4

Chapter 2.   WordPress   7

    Responsiveness   8
    Search Engine Optimization (SEO)   8
    Multiple Languages   9

Website Analytics   9

Security   9

Default Themes   10

Chapter 3.   **Thesis Theme**   **11**

Skin Management   16

Skin Content   17

Skin Design   20

Header Image   21

Skin Editor   22

Custom CSS   34

Manage Skins   36

Manage Boxes   38

The Site Menu   39

Chapter 4.   **The Best Plugins—Part 1 Simple Tasks**   **43**

How to Install and Activate a Plugin   45

Akismet   47

Email Subscribers   49

Testimonial Rotator   51

Simple Social Icons   53

Two Column Admin   54

Custom Sidebars   55

TinyMCE Color picker   56

Store Locator Plus   57

WP Currency Converter   60

OpenHook   60

WP Clone   63

FileBrowser   65

Simple Maintenance   66

Add From Server   66

WordPress Popup   68

Simple Links   69

Easy Twitter Feed Widget (Other Social Feeds)   70

Chapter 5. The Best Plugins—Part 2 Advanced Tasks   73

Wordfence Security   74

Google Analytics Dashboard for WP   76

Contact Form 7 / Contact Form DB   80

Master Slider   86

WooCommerce   89

Yoast SEO   94

WP eMember ($)   98

Backup Scheduler   100

Inline Google Spreadsheet Viewer   101

Chapter 6. Other Resources   107

Online Resources   107

Troubleshooting Assistance   110

Finding a Great Host   112

The Community   112

Table of Contents

This book is dedicated to the WordPress and PHP communities. These people are amazing, friendly, and giving. You know what "community" truly means and you live it every day. I have personally met hundreds of people that strive each day to make these products and therefore the world better. Keep on doing what you do best!

Acknowledgments

I want to thank my wife, Dawn once again for inspiring me to write yet another book. Of course, thanks also to php[architect] for publishing this book; Oscar and Eli saw the potential here and pounced on it. For the editors and graphics folks who make my babblings coherent, and for Eric Mann for his great introduction. Also, Cory Gallant for helping me into the WordPress world.

Cheers, Peter MacIntyre

BUILDING EXCEPTIONAL SITES WITH WORDPRESS & THESIS

Foreword

In late 2007, I was trying to build a custom registration platform for a friend's online course. He wanted to track which salesperson had recruited a student, and was depending on me to make the magic happen. The biggest downside to the arrangement: I had no idea where to even begin with such a feature. The course system was running on a platform I'd never heard of: WordPress. I knew that the platform supported "plugins" and "themes" but had no clue how to get started building out the features my friend needed. I searched the Internet, scoured the how-to section of my local bookstore, and asked various "experts" who frequented a local user group.

What I realized was that getting started with WordPress was *hard*. The WordPress ecosystem was, at the time, entirely new ground for many developers. It took great, concerted effort to find the right tools. To meet the right people. To even define and understand the terms and buzzwords used within the community. This struggle is endemic to learning *any* new technology, but when contrasted with the "ease of use" heralded by WordPress, it can become even more intimidating.

The power behind WordPress is that it's open and the community is typically more than willing to help answer questions. The open-source nature of the platform means anyone with a text editor can get their hands dirty and actually work with the code. It's well documented, easy to learn, and so popular that it powers more than a quarter of the Internet! Unfortunately, it also means a Google search for the best starting point with WordPress can return literally *thousands* of results regardless of how the question is phrased.

Fortunately, it's no longer 2007. Starting out with WordPress no longer means scouring Google, spending hours at the bookstore, or trolling user groups. WordPress itself has become a remarkably easy-to-configure platform for basic sites. Themes like Thesis extend WordPress to make it an even more powerful platform—and all of the configuration happens in the site itself! No more hacking at code in a text editor!

If you're just getting started, *Building Exceptional Sites with WordPress & Thesis* will walk you through everything you need to set up your new site and hit the ground running with the best tools in the industry. If your site is already up, the book then serves as a handy go-to manual to keep everything running at peak efficiency. I've been working professionally with WordPress for nine years and can honestly say I would have been more productive on Day One had this book been available.

Wherever you are on your journey with WordPress and site development, it's handy to have at least one resource you can come back to when you hit a snag. This is that book. Best of luck with your next WordPress/Thesis project!

Eric Mann,
@ericmann
April 2016

FOREWORD

Chapter

1

Requirements

HTML & CSS

This book is based on a basic understanding of both HTML and CSS (Cascading Style Sheets) mark up. If you are not well versed in these technologies, then please use your favorite search engine for assistance. W3 Schools[1] and Mozilla's Developer Network[2] are great places to start and of course there are many books out there to consider picking up and going through.

Environments

Before we get into the nitty-gritty of WordPress and Thesis we need to discuss the broader topic of development environments versus production environments and how to install these great solutions onto each of these platforms.

There are a few schools of thought on how many environments are really needed; from development, to staging, to production. Development is where you add new features to your project and try them out. It is a volatile environment where you can experiment with ideas and should really have no inhibitions when it comes to trying things out. The staging platform is a place where you can push your new ideas to a select group of reviewers and testers to prove what

[1]   W3 Schools: http://www.w3schools.com
[2]   Mozilla Developer Network: https://developer.mozilla.org/en-US/is

Environments **FIGURE 1.1**

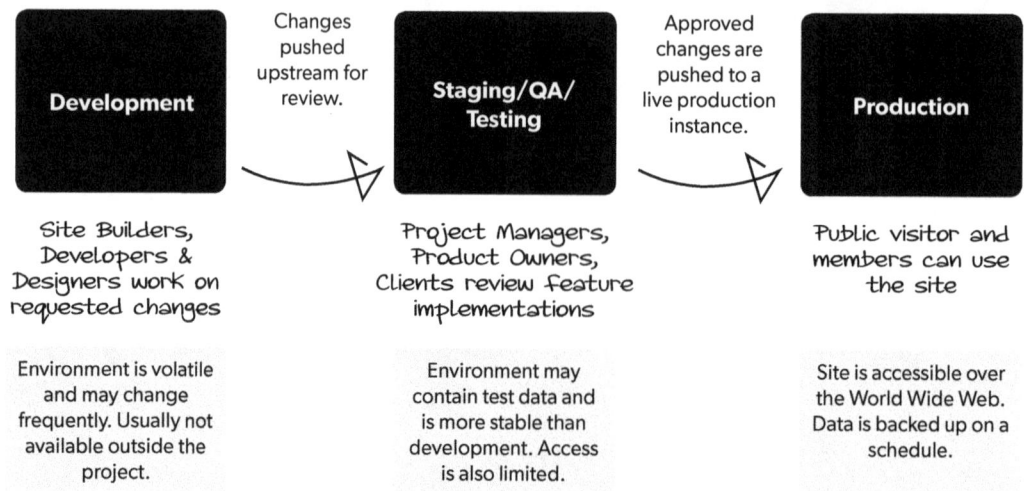

Development	Changes pushed upstream for review.	Staging/QA/ Testing	Approved changes are pushed to a live production instance.	Production

Site Builders, Developers & Designers work on requested changes

Project Managers, Product Owners, Clients review feature implementations

Public visitor and members can use the site

Environment is volatile and may change frequently. Usually not available outside the project.

Environment may contain test data and is more stable than development. Access is also limited.

Site is accessible over the World Wide Web. Data is backed up on a schedule.

you have done in your experimental environment will actually work; it meets any agreed upon requirements and can be accepted before you release it to the entire world. Production is the platform where your live, publicly accessible site is served. At the very least you should have a development platform separate from your live production environment. You certainly don't want to attempt to use a new plugin and go through some time in set up on your live site.

So given the bare minimum of development and production platforms, you may be asking *where* these environments should be hosted. You may think this should go without saying but it must be said: try your absolute best to have the platforms (their underlying technologies—PHP, MySQL, Web server, and WordPress) of both environments as identical as possible. You may not have this ideal development environment of multiple identical platforms available to you, or you may want to develop in your favorite operating system and deploy to a different operating system platform for production. You may want to develop on your local desktop environment for speed and convenience rather than depend on the environment of the production host. But keep in mind, the more different these environments are from each other, the greater the chance is for grief and lost time hunting down the causes of bugs.

If you don't develop on the same operating system as your staging and production environments, you should research the differences between your OS and the target OS. Differences may exist between case-sensitivity for file and directory names and the PHP extensions available on each.

As you can see the options are many and varied. Here are some helpful links to guide you in setting up a hosting platform regardless of the physical location. Each of these has the aim of providing a means to easily install all the software components needed to run and serve a WordPress environment. You would, however, still need to install WordPress on top of these environments.

Of course there is no need to do this if you are using a hosting platform which caters to WordPress sites.

MAMP

MAMP stands for Mac (operating system which is actually OS X), Apache (web server software), MySQL (database server), PHP (web development language). WordPress is built with PHP. Typically, this is installed on a Mac for local development, hosting on a OS X is fairly rare. The WordPress Codex has instructions for *Installing WordPress Locally on Your Mac With MAMP*[3]

LAMP

LAMP stands for Linux (operating system; usually a distribution of it like Ubuntu, Debian, Red Hat, etc.), Apache (web server software), MySQL (database software), PHP (Web development language). If you search for WordPress and your distribution, you'll find articles like WordPress on Debian Linux[4]

WAMP

WAMP stands for Windows (operating system), Apache (web server software), MySQL (database software), PHP (web development language). WampDeveloper Pro[5] provides a paid stack to install on Windows machines:

For a more generic discussion on development environments, visit WordPress' Developer page on *Setting up a Development Environment*[6].

As a final note to this environment discussion, you can use the concept of subdomains to perform development before setting up a production site. So for example, if the production destination of a WordPress site is going to be river-thames.com then on a development server we would create this sub-domain: riverthames.paladin-bs-dev.com. If you control the DNS settings for the domain, you could even use dev.river-thames.com.

Having both environments on the same web hosting platform like Bluehost or GoDaddy would be the ideal. This also lends itself well to moving content from development to production (deployment) as folders, file names, and file locations would all be similar, if not identical.

[3] *Installing WordPress Locally on Your Mac With MAMP*: http://phpa.me/wp-install-mamp
[4] *WordPress on Debian Linux*: http://supriyadisw.net/?p=319
[5] *WampDeveloperPro*: http://www.devside.net/howto/wordpress-manual-install
[6] *Setting up a Development Environment*: https://developer.wordpress.org/?p=5806

WordPress Install

WordPress touts their five minute installation process[7] but there is a little more to setting up WordPress than that. Getting the right configuration and default plugins is also nice to have ready to go. Unless you are in a mad rush to get WordPress up and running, consider the following more calculated approach.

Let's assume you've set up your hosting environment and have an administration account for securely connecting to the platform's FTP access and have downloaded the basic install files for WordPress. You are ready to set up the WordPress environment in a default way. By this we mean having all the files and plugins you regularly use across sites ready to be uploaded. See Figure 1.2 for the listing of a standard WordPress file structure.

> *We're using FTP in a generic sense. Plain FTP is not a secure protocol, make sure you are using FTP over TLS, SFTP, or another protocol that is encrypted. This is especially important to protect files with sensitive information like database credentials or API keys.*

Here you will see the folder called WordPress_43 [1] where a basic install is kept. After a basic installation is done and (in our opinion) useless default plugins like "Hello Dolly" are removed, we installed two plugins we employ on every development environment: Akismet and WP clone [2]. See *Chapter 4* for details on these two plugins. Then, we re-connect (via secure FTP) to the host and download the entire WordPress file structure. Now we have the default installation we want with our desired pre-loaded plugins already installed. We can then upload this file structure as often as we need to for each subsequent WordPress project.

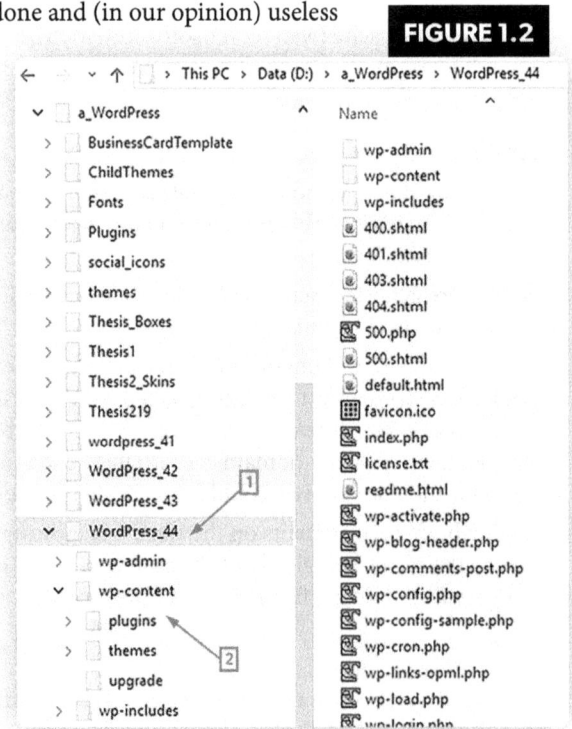

FIGURE 1.2

wp-config Settings

After you have uploaded your new default files, the next thing you should do is edit the WordPress configuration file wp-config.php to allow WordPress to connect to the database you will be using on your host for each installation. The database name and admin accesses are set up ahead of time on the hosting

[7]   Famous 5-Minute Install: http://phpa.me/wp-5minute

platform or by your system administrator. If you can, edit this file after you upload it to the server. If you can't edit it on the server then make the changes locally and upload the file after you save your changes. Regardless, make the following changes to this file:

FIGURE 1.3

```
16
17   // ** MySQL settings - You can get this info from your web host ** //
18   /** The name of the database for WordPress */
19   define('DB_NAME', 'pa▒▒▒▒_▒▒▒ha');          1
20
21   /** MySQL database username */
22   define('DB_USER', 'pa▒▒▒#_▒▒in');           2
23
24   /** MySQL database password */
25   define('DB_PASSWORD', '1▒▒▒▒▒▒▒Q');          3
26
27   /** MySQL hostname */
28   define('DB_HOST', 'localhost');
29
30   /** Increase Memory for WordPress */
31   define( 'WP_MEMORY_LIMIT', '64M' );          4
32
33   /** Database Charset to use in creating database tables. */
34   define('DB_CHARSET', 'utf8');
35
36   /** The Database Collate type. Don't change this if in doubt. */
37   define('DB_COLLATE', '');
38
39   define('FTP_HOST', 'f▒▒▒▒▒bs.com');          5
40   define('FTP_USER', 'a▒▒▒▒▒n-bs.com');
41   define('FTP_PASS', '1▒▒▒▒▒Q');
```

1. Provide the name of the database you will be using on this host.
2. Provide the name of the database user account which has access to the named database on this host.
3. Provide the password of the database user account which has access to the named database on this host.
4. If you want to attempt to increase the memory usage of the default installation of PHP on your server (if you are using a commercial host like Bluehost or GoDaddy), try to enact the setting of WP_MEMORY_LIMIT and set it to 64M. This will allow your site to better handle page loading, and therefore, serve your site visitors more quickly. The usual default is 8M or 16M. Be aware, some hosts will curtail this option and you won't be allowed to alter this value, but it's always worth it to attempt to change this value for your sites responsiveness.
5. If you don't want to be asked every time you add or update a plugin on your site, also make the changes for FTP access in this configuration file.

Save your changes and then open a browser to run the WordPress setup routines of your new site. This is done by simply calling the location of your site and WordPress will recognize it has never been setup before and will run its install scripts. With our example above on the development environment you would simply type in the following URL: `riverthames.paladin-bs-dev.com`. In your browser, you should see something similar to Figure 1.4, where the language selection is offered to you as the first step in the setup process.

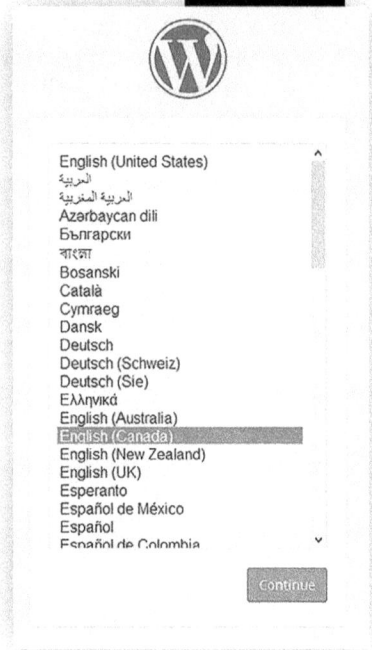

FIGURE 1.4

Autoupdate (Yea or Nay?)

As of WordPress version 3.7, the built-in, automatic update process was added to the core of the product. This means any updates for maintenance or security reasons will automatically be performed when the WordPress Development team releases them. Other major updates, like full version updates (from version 3 to 4 for example) will still be at the user's (your own) control and discretion. You can over-ride this feature if you want, but for your own self-preservation you should seriously consider the ramifications of disabling this process. Plugins (except where they may affect the overall security of a WordPress site) will always be left for you to upgrade manually. See the discussion on Wordfence in *Chapter 5* for some help on getting notified when updates are pending.

If you do want to over-ride this functionality you can simply add a directive to the `wp-config.php` file like this:

```
define('AUTOMATIC_UPDATER_DISABLED', true);
```

The above will completely disable all updates on the site. If you want to be more precise in what you allow for updates you can use the following directive:

```
define('WP_AUTO_UPDATE_CORE', false);
```

The second option has three possible values: `false`, `true`, or `minor`. `True` means major, minor, and development updates are enabled (you would have to be using a development version of WordPress for this to have an effect on developmental features). On other sites this means major and minor CORE updates only are automatically updated. False means major, minor, and developmental updates are disabled. Minor means only minor updates will be updated and both developmental and major CORE updates will be disabled.

For a full discussion on this topic and all its nuances read *Configuring Automatic Background Updates*[8]

[8]   *Configuring Automatic Background Updates:* http://phpa.me/wp-autoupdate-config

Chapter 2

WordPress

The needs of a website these days is quite a daunting topic to broach. When approaching your needs, you have to be very specific in what you want your site to do and who will be its audience. This chapter will discuss websites in a broader sense, to get you thinking along these lines. We hope to help you answer some of the following questions:

1. What do I want my website to do?
2. What will my website look like?
3. Who will be my audience?
4. Where will my audience be located?
5. How will I reach my audience?
6. How will my audience find me?
7. How will I communicate with my audience?
8. How do I keep my site's content up to date?
9. How do I protect my content?
10. Do I leverage social media for my site?
11. How do I know if I am accomplishing my goals for my site?
12. Will others be accessing my site as an administrator, or just me?
13. Do I want to sell anything on my site?

This is just a short list of questions which will get you to start really considering what you want your web presence to be and do. In the following sections we will explore how WordPress can and does have the ability to answer some of these questions. Depending on the theme and your selected plugins you can answer all of these questions but keep in mind that "how" you want these questions answered is just as important. Also, depending on how these questions are resolved may well determine what plugins and themes you will employ on your site.

When you're thinking of features your site will provide, it is better to focus on what business problems you need to solve rather than in prescribing exactly **how** to solve them. You may find a plugin which provides a different workflow or user interface you can use to accomplish your goals, instead of getting stuck in the depths of attempting to code and implement your own custom prescribed solution. So be sure to look around at different plugins which may only be partially described as solving your use requirement; with a little thinking and alternative use it may end up completely filling your need in the end.

Responsiveness

This is likely the largest and most important question which needs to be addressed in relation to your website. Responsiveness means your website's design adjusts to what type of device your visitors are using and will adjust its presentation display automatically. Typically, this means checking the screen size and changing elements like font-sizes, image sizes, and how content flows on the page. iPhone (portrait), iPhone (landscape), iPad (portrait), iPad (landscape), Samsung Galaxy phones, Blackberry phones, desktop monitors; these are just a few of the many devices available to the public and chances are your site visitors will be using at least two of these (if not more) to view your site. Not long ago websites were designed for the desktop with mobile device display as an afterthought, if it was considered at all.

More recently, websites are—or should be—designed for mobility first and desktop viewing, second. Be sure your WordPress theme can handle responsive design and it is clearly mentioned in its descriptive text. This does not fully guarantee your site will look fantastic on all devices, but it will at least give you a foundation of responsiveness from which to commence the creation of your website. Full responsiveness is then controlled with custom CSS (cascading style sheets). Typically, a desktop view of your site will look fairly different than the mobile version due to screen real estate and desired functionality. Make sure you or your web developer knows what they are doing in this respect. This will answer question number two in our list above.

Search Engine Optimization (SEO)

Search Engine Optimization (SEO) is a well-honed skill unto itself. SEO is the use of meta (embedded) keywords and descriptions which help search engines like Google and Bing to find and include your website on the list of returned search items when someone performs a search. There are entire companies specializing in this one aspect of web design alone. What you do with SEO will answer questions five and six above. Chapter 5 has a section on the *SEO plugin by Yoast* so be sure to study that section as you plan for ways to get discovered. Thesis has a few rudimentary SEO features namely in **Site** > **Blog Page SEO** but it is very limited in the grand scheme of SEO in comparison to what the Yoast plugin provides.

Multiple Languages

Answering question number three will dictate if you need a multi-language website. We don't cover multi-language issues in this book as it is well beyond our scope, but it certainly demands a short discussion here when you're going through the content and design phases of building your website. If you decide you want to be a multi-language, site be sure to check out the "xili-language" plugin[1]. There are many issues to cover here like menu wording, page naming, languages to support, duplicating content, SEO for each language, and so on that you'll have to take into consideration.

Website Analytics

One of the most valuable aspects of hosting a website is the ability to see who has accessed your site, from where they did this, and the frequency of visits. Enter Google Analytics. This free Google tool is invaluable for guiding your marketing and sales thrusts for your site (if marketing and sales are indeed important to you). The statistics Google Analytics provides will also allow you to fine tune your efforts and adjust your SEO if and when needed. Chapter 5 has a section on the plugin called *Google Analytics Dashboard for WP*. So be sure to look into this plugin. Again, Thesis has some rudimentary tie-ins to Google Analytics if you don't want to use the previously mentioned plugin. See **Site > Google Analytics**. Attention to the Google Analytics information will help to answer question number eleven.

Google Analytics is popular because it's free, although you are giving Google insight into your site visitors. There are alternatives for website analytics and many will have a WordPress plugin or some JavaScript code to enable data collection.

Security

Question number nine is vital no matter what your site is meant for. To have a site as secure as possible is very important indeed. You don't want to be hacked and you don't want your content to suddenly be tainted in way disparaging to your image or what you want to portray to the Internet world. In WordPress there are basically two types of vulnerabilities.

The first part of site protection is more general in coverage. You can be attacked in many ways, some as simple as a malicious user correctly guessing your administration password. *Wordfence* is a good free security plugin and is discussed in chapter 5. Two other plugins to be considered if you need to be extra secure are iThemes Security[2] (commercial) and BruteProtect[3] (part of the Jetpack multi-plug-in)! These plugins keep a running list of site vulnerabilities and also keep a watch out for site attacks by humans or code-bots. They can even alert you by email and block the IP addresses of attempts to guess your passwords, or exploit known insecure plugins, etc.

[1]   xili-language: *https://wordpress.org/plugins/xili-language/*
[2]   iThemes Security: *https://ithemes.com/security/*
[3]   BruteProtect: *http://bruteprotect.com*

Another aspect to site security is the administration area which is typically accessed with paths prefixed by /wp-admin. Since this is a standard to WordPress it can be an access point for security breaches. Consider using the plugin called *Protect Your Admin* to re-direct your admin login URL to a location you name yourself like "secret_admin_login" or whatever you like, but pick something not easily guessable. This will only allow login access to the admin area to real people who are aware of this re-named URL.

Comment Spam

The second type of issue you can face is un-wanted comments to your posts–comment spam. This may not be a "real" security risk, but it's damn annoying. To control this, you can simply either turn off comments site-wide or force comments to be approved by the site administrators. See **Settings > Discussion** for options on this. If you do want to allow comments and site feedback, but want to filter it you can use the *Akismet plugin* to help with filtering spam submissions. Chapter 4 has a section covering this plugin and its value.

Default Themes

WordPress comes with a few default themes which are updated often and have some nice features. WordPress names their themes after the year they are released. So you may see themes called *Twenty Fourteen* and *Twenty Fifteen*. These themes are great for getting started with WordPress or if you only want a very basic site which doesn't need a lot of additional features. Of course, we think Thesis is one of the best and most versatile themes existing on the WordPress market, which is why this book was written.

Chapter 3

Thesis Theme

Throw a stone and you will hit a WordPress theme. At the time of this writing, there are over 1,880 active free themes for download from *http://wordpress.org*. Add to that the countless commercial themes on the market and you have almost as confusing a theme world as you do a plugin world.

With so many options, how is one to navigate through all the "noise" to find a theme platform they can work well within and which is flexible enough to be bent beyond its common use? We have collectively used many themes; some free and some commercial, and although we have certainly not used them all, when we found Thesis, we fell in love! To use a song title from the 1980's rock band Survivor: *The Search is Over*.

In this chapter we will attempt to show you why and how we think Thesis is one of the premier WordPress themes on the market today. Notice we said "on the market"? Thesis is a commercial theme, but in our opinion is well worth the modest fees they charge. If you visit *http://diythemes.com/plans* you can see their three-tiered fee structure. The professional version is the one with all the bells and whistles, so if you can justify the cost (currently US$197) it is money well spent. You're bound to recoup it once you save a few hours of work and headaches.

Installation

Let's get started with Thesis by installing it. As of this writing, the current version is 2.2 and your WordPress version should be 4.4 or newer. Once you purchase and download Thesis as a zip file simply go to **Appearance > Themes** and click **Add New**, then click on **Upload Theme**; navigate to the location of your downloaded zip file, select it, and then click **Install Now**. Make sure you activate the theme if it doesn't automatically activate itself. You should see Thesis added to the left navigation menu shown in figure 3.1 (the full sub-menu is showing as well).

Basic Layout

The basic interface for navigating in Thesis can take some getting used to. As shown in Figure 3.1 you can get to the top level tasks within Thesis by way of the left side admin area. However, once you are within Thesis there is a complementary menu available at the top of the page. This allows for access to additional features and functions in the theme. So, if you sometimes find yourself a little lost when looking for a feature be sure to look in both menu areas. Figure 3.2 shows the skin menu pulled down for item selection.

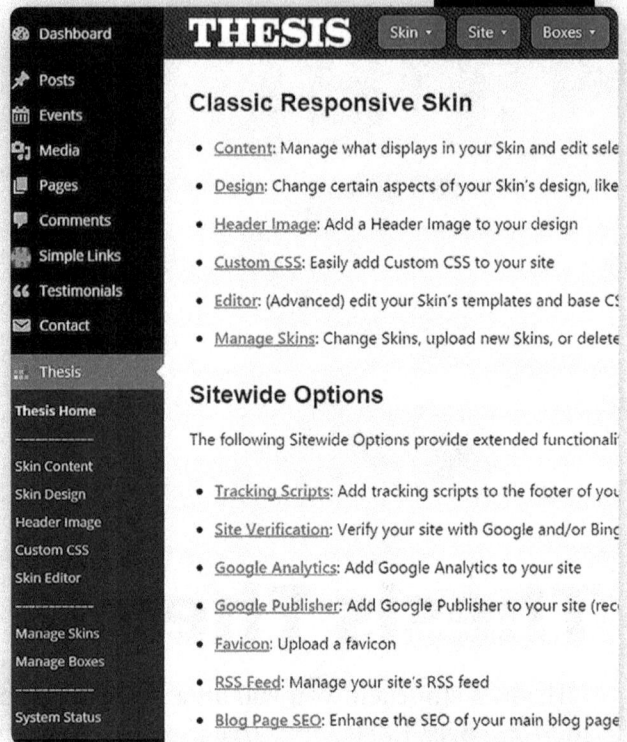

FIGURE 3.1

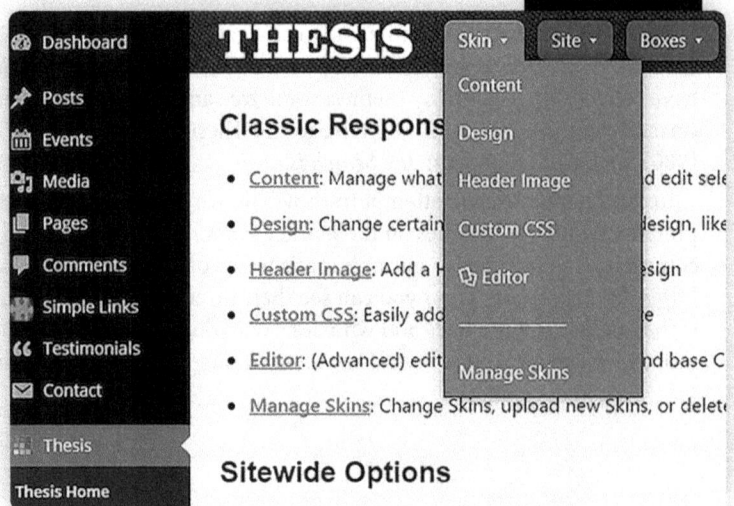

FIGURE 3.2

Also, note there is yet another menu on the far right of the Thesis display which can be used for peripheral matters like checking what version you have, adding your license key, and accessing the online user guide.

FIGURE 3.3

If you have purchased the latest version of the Thesis theme and have a license key. You would add it in this screen. See Figure 3.3 for what this form looks like.

Basic Concepts

So what is Thesis anyway? In a few words it is both a theme design tool and a theme page template manager. This is a tricky concept to get across and understand if you are used to using a single theme for every page on your other WordPress sites. Thesis has a basic concept they call *skins*. The skin has two parts which need to be understood in order to gain complete understanding about its many uses.

First, Thesis provides skins for use within its theme in the way you can think of as a sub-theme. Their *Classic Responsive Skin* is the one automatically installed when you first set up Thesis. If you purchase the professional version, then you also have access to two additional skins: *Promo* and *Personified*. Each of these skins has different layouts and a slightly different presentation of the content on your site. To see what each skin looks like you can either simply switch to the skin on your own site. Figures 3.4, 3.5, and 3.6 show the themes when this book was prepared. For the most recent samples visit the website here: *http://diythemes.com/demo/*. You can easily switch between the skins here to see what they would look like and to select the one that you want to use.

FIGURE 3.4

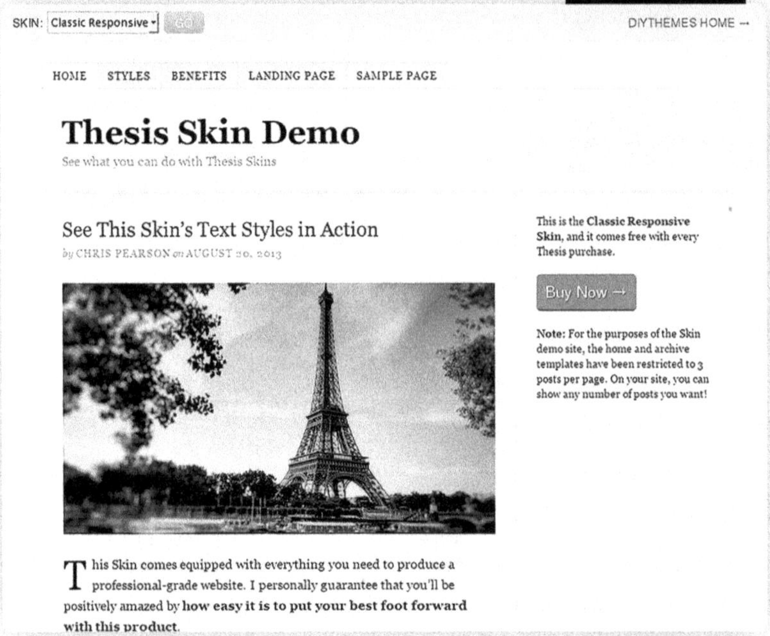

FIGURE 3.5

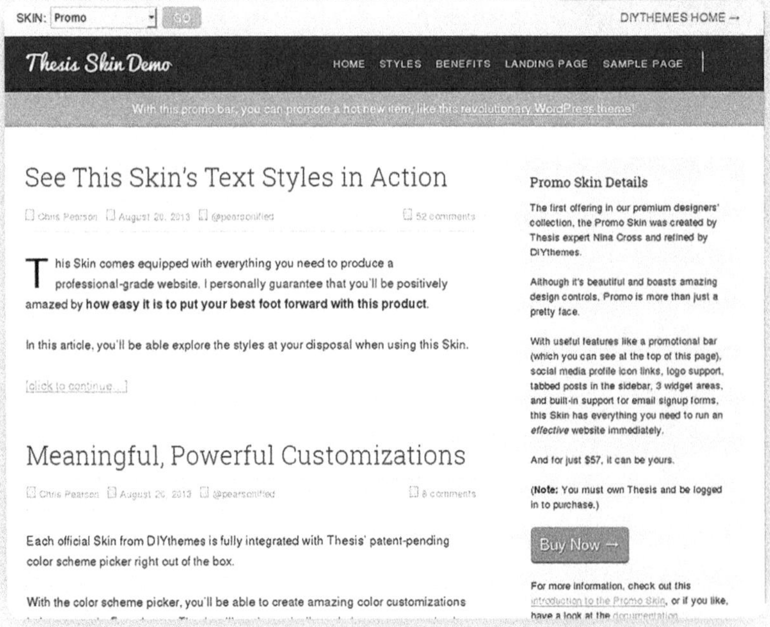

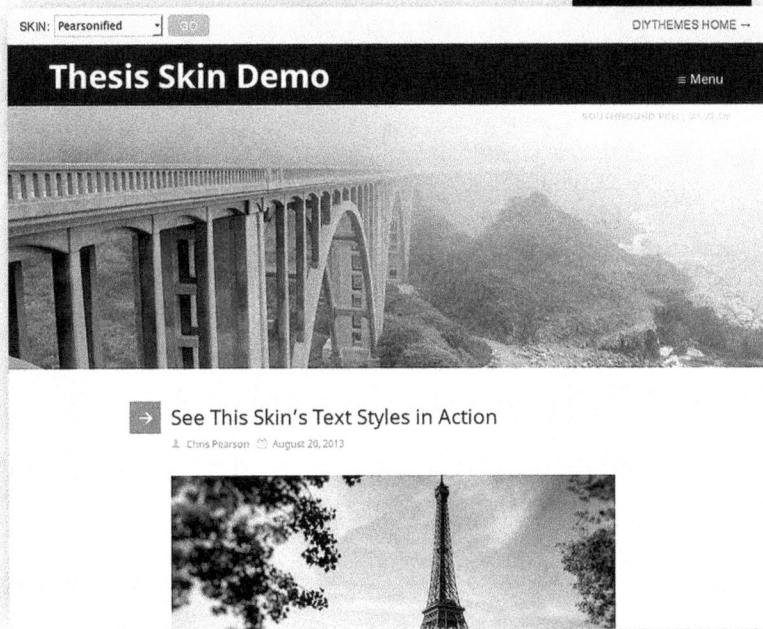

FIGURE 3.6

Once you have these skins installed (we will show you how to do this in the following paragraphs), you can switch between these skins to see totally different web page layouts at the click of a mouse.

*Thesis has a Developer's Toolbox paid Professional licenses have access to. This tool can be installed in the **Thesis** > **Manage Boxes** page. This toolbox has the ability to export your designs as individual skins. Once installed there is a new menu option added to the Boxes menu called **Thesis Dev Tools**. With this tool you can use the skin editor to create something new and then export it to the world as your own custom skin. There are many of these custom skins on the web (found by using Google), but none of them are "sanctioned" by DIY Themes (the makers of Thesis). Documentation for this toolbox is on the DIY Theme website under the user's signed in account.*

Secondly, Thesis has a "Skin Editor" which allows you the ability to change the layout and look and feel of individual pages within each skin. These are also known as "Page Templates". So, for example, you could have different page layouts and designs for your site individual pages like "About", "Contact Us", and so on; and a totally different layout for your blog pages and again a different layout for your homepage. Let's look at the skin management area now starting with how to install a skin.

Skin Management

In the admin menu, select the following menu path: **Thesis > Manage Skins**. You will be taken to the skin management page. Here you can click on the blue button in the top right of the screen called **Upload Skin**. Skin file decks should have been previously downloaded zip files which will be located, uploaded, and installed in the same manner as the Thesis theme was installed. You will see an overlay screen like that shown in Figure 3.7.

FIGURE 3.7

Upload a Thesis Skin   OK

Choose File | promo.zip

Add Skin

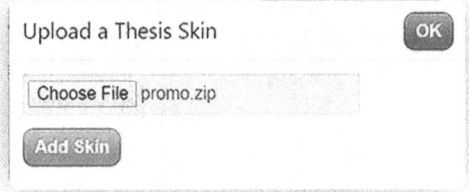

Select the skin zip file and click on the **Add Skin** button. The skin files will be added to the Thesis theme. Figure 3.8 shows the addition of the *Promo* skin having been added to the skin management area.

FIGURE 3.8

Current Skin

Classic Responsive v 1.2 *by* Chris Pearson

Elegant and versatile, the Classic Responsive Skin features clean lines and mathematical precision with an emphasis on typography.

Classic
RESPONSIVE
minimalist design with
Golden Ratio Typography

Inactive Skins

Upload a New Skin

Promo v 1.2 *by* Nina Cross and DIYthemes

A responsive, content-focused Skin with unlimited color schemes, a promo bar for catching visitors' attention, a tabbed posts widget, social media profile icon links, and more!

Preview Skin in Development Mode

Activate Skin   Delete Skin

Promo

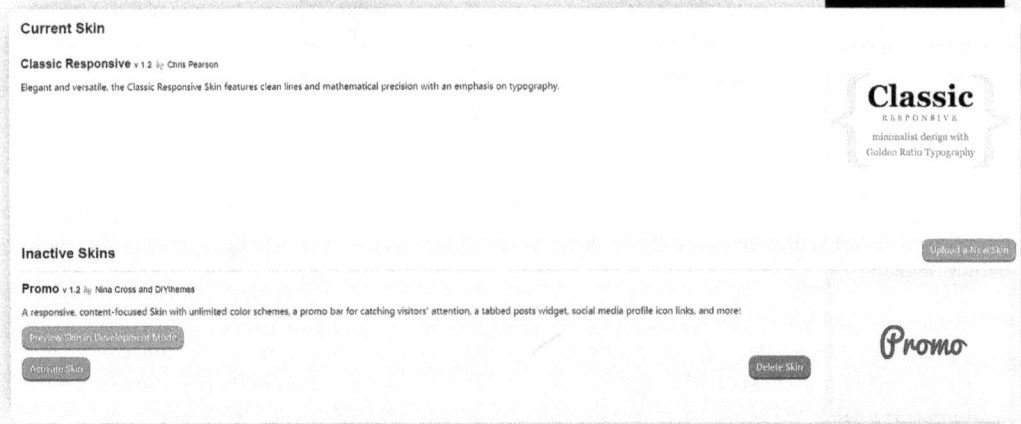

To switch between active skins, simply click on the green *Activate Skin* button for the skin you want and the switch will be made instantly. The other options on this page are self-explanatory. These are **Delete Skin** (it has to be inactive) and **Preview Skin in Development Mode**—this allows you to see your site within the preview context of the selected skin without switching to it on your live publicly accessible site. Be sure to go back and deactivate the preview when you are done with it so you aren't confused between the active skin and the preview skin.

The next few menu items within the Thesis admin area may take some time to get used to. It is best to read these sections over and play with them within your own development environment as you read along, so you can practice and get familiar with them at the same time.

There are two menu items which will be discussed together next, as they basically go hand-in-hand as you explore skin management manipulation.

Skin Content

Click on **Thesis > Skin Content** in the admin menu or **Skin > Content** in the pull down menu. You will be taken to the page shown in Figure 3.9. There are two major areas of interest on this page *Display Options* and *Skin Content*.

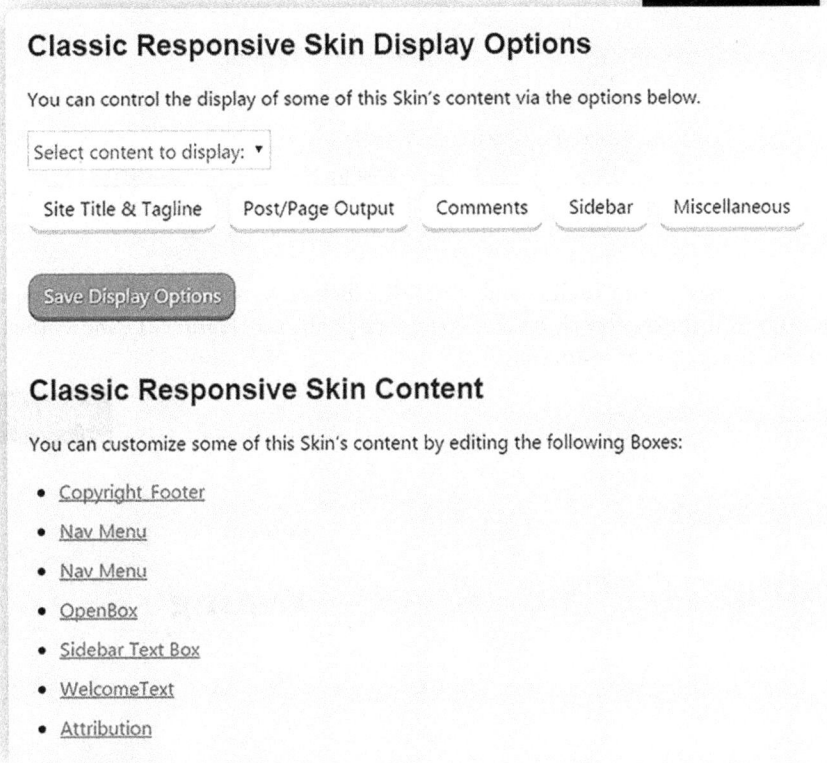

FIGURE 3.9

Classic Responsive Skin Display Options

You can control the display of some of this Skin's content via the options below.

Select content to display: ▾

Site Title & Tagline   Post/Page Output   Comments   Sidebar   Miscellaneous

Save Display Options

Classic Responsive Skin Content

You can customize some of this Skin's content by editing the following Boxes:

- Copyright Footer
- Nav Menu
- Nav Menu
- OpenBox
- Sidebar Text Box
- WelcomeText
- Attribution

We will be doing all our work in this chapter within the Classic Responsive Skin. *If you're using another skin like* Promo *or* Personified *these pages may look slightly different.*

Keeping in mind a skin is like a sub-theme to Thesis, it is here you can control what is included or excluded from the skin when sections of your site are displayed to the public. You are presented with five buttons which each activate pop-up overlays or dialog windows. Here, you can simply select the check-boxes beside the content you want to control. As an example, we will be turning off the site tagline. Click on the **Site Title & Tagline** button. You will see the screen shown in Figure 3.10.

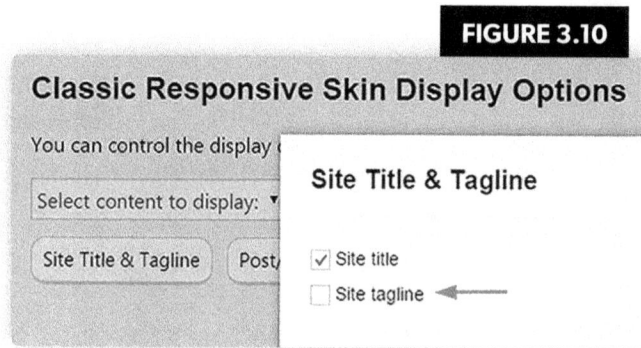

FIGURE 3.10

Uncheck the box beside **Site Tagline** and click **OK**. Click on **Save Display Options** on the right of the page after the overlay closes and go to your public site. Figure 3.11 shows the before and after of this change to our testing site.

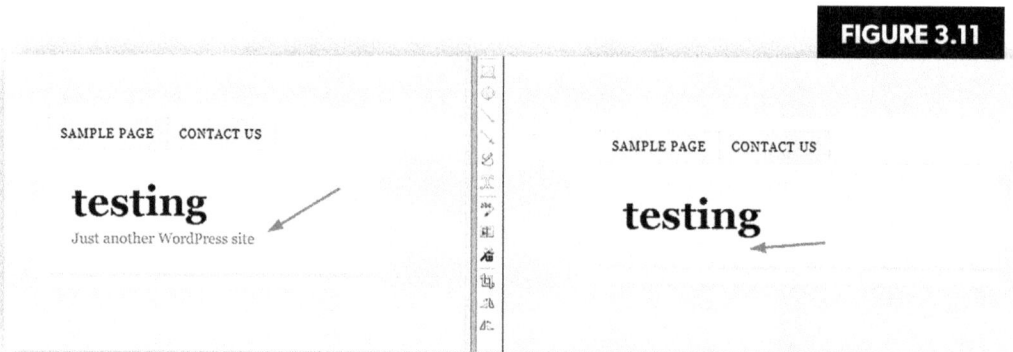

FIGURE 3.11

Take some time to explore all the options within the four other buttons in the *Display Options* area in the content section. Some of the toggles which can be turned on or off may not be readily visible depending on the detail design you employ in the skin editor, but more on that later.

In the bottom half of the content page you'll see a list of links like *Copyright Footer*, *Nav Menu*, and so on. These links are provided by default as part of the active skin, but you can control the details of each of those topics. For example, if you checked on *Nav Menu* you will be taken to a page where you can select which menu you want to use in this skin if you have more than one menu defined within WordPress under the **Appearance > Menus** section. Still, others like **Sidebar Text Box** will open an HTML editor screen when clicked. Here you can add any HTML or text to the sidebar area and it will be used throughout your site. As shown in Figure 3.12, we simply put some basic HTML in the editor and saved it.

The display of the public site now looks like that in Figure 3.13.

Remember, our sidebar is on the left side of our layout in our example website. The *Attribution* text is used in the footer of the pages excluding the footer of the home page in the skin. You can override this text with the *Attribution* link here as well. The "Copyright Footer" link has a similar effect on the home page.

As you add HTML/Open boxes to your own skin's edited pages, this list of links will grow and your customization of the skin will expand accordingly. More on how this is done will be described in the "Skin Editor" section later in this chapter.

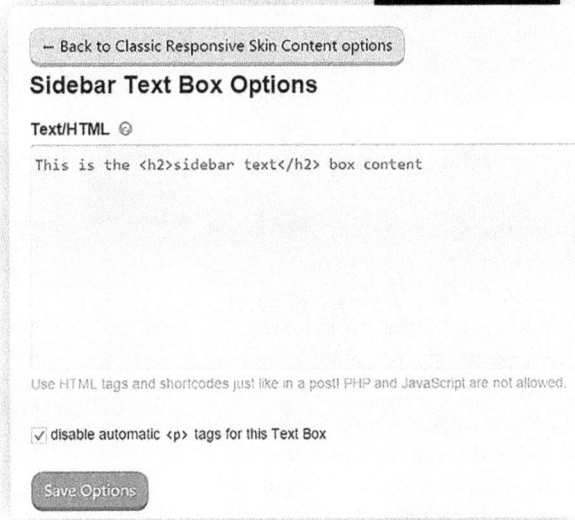

FIGURE 3.12

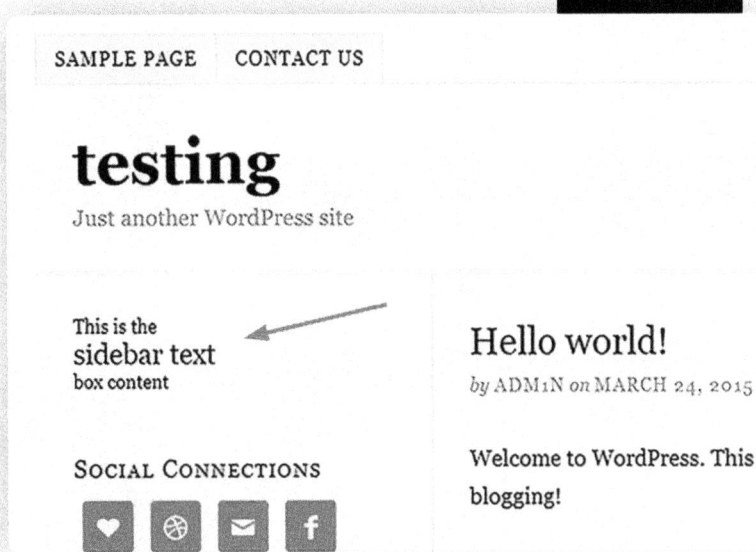

FIGURE 3.13

Skin Design

The *Skin Design* page, accessed by **Thesis > Skin Design** or **Skin > Design** in the pull down menu, looks like the screen capture shown in Figure 3.14.

Here on this page you can control the color theme of your site in fine detail. A color selector is provided for Primary Text, Secondary Text, Links, Borders, and Highlights, as well as Interior Backgrounds (BGs) and Site BG. Figure 3.15 shows many of the ways in which you can wield that control.

For each major category of site design mentioned above, you can specifically control their individual colors. If you hover your mouse over the top right corner of the color box [2] you will see a pop-up of potentially complementary colors to the overall scheme currently being used [1]. If you want to directly control the Hex values of the color box, you can click your mouse in the middle of the box and change the alphanumeric codes [3]. At the same time, a drop-down color selector will appear [4] to assist you in the selection. But probably of greatest value is what happens when you click on the **Thesis Color Scale** button [5]. Another color selection box opens and you can select from a wide range of color pallets

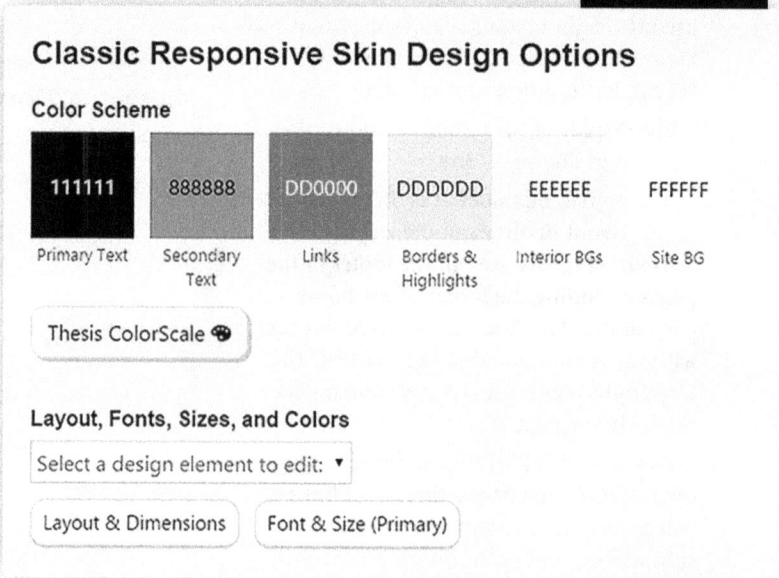

FIGURE 3.14

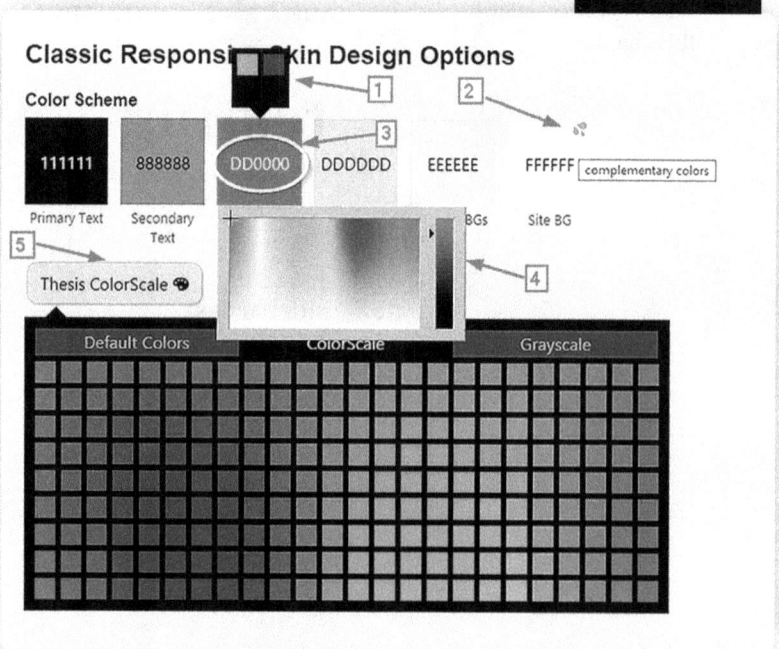

FIGURE 3.15

which will affect the whole color scheme of the website. If you wanted to select an overall theme of complementary colors this is one way to accomplish it.

You can also control the font sizes on a site-wide basis and can even designate a different font (with attributes) per section of the site using the provided drop-down selector under the heading of *Layout, Fonts, Sizes, and Colors*. If, for example, you wanted the post headlines of your blog entries to be different than your default font values, simply select **Headlines** and a dialogue opens allowing you to make adjustments. Figures 3.16 and 3.17 show this being done.

Don't forget to click on **Save Design Options** to secure any changes you make on this page.

Header Image

As the name suggests, this is the location where you can add an image to your homepage. Accessed by **Thesis > Header Image** or **Skin > Header Image** in the pull down menu. The image should be of a banner style so it takes up the full width of the designated screen real estate. Take note, if an image is selected and saved here the site name and tagline text are superseded by this image. The image can be sourced from your existing media library or uploaded from an external source. Figure 3.18 shows a selected header image.

FIGURE 3.16

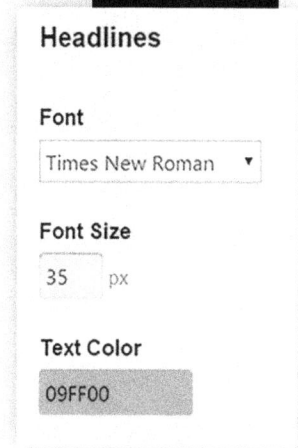

FIGURE 3.17

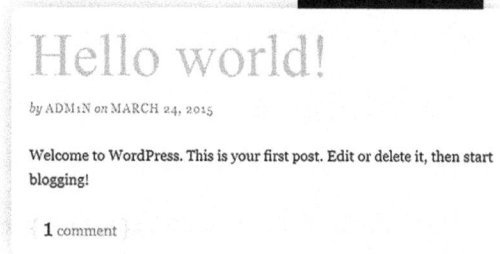

FIGURE 3.18

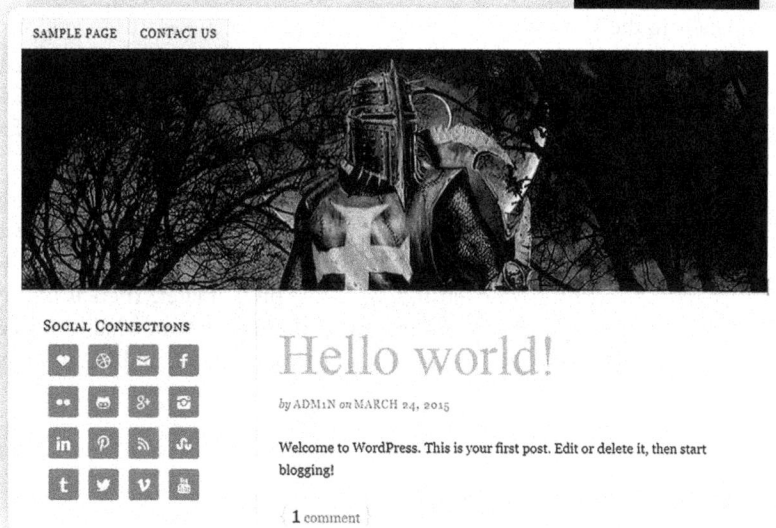

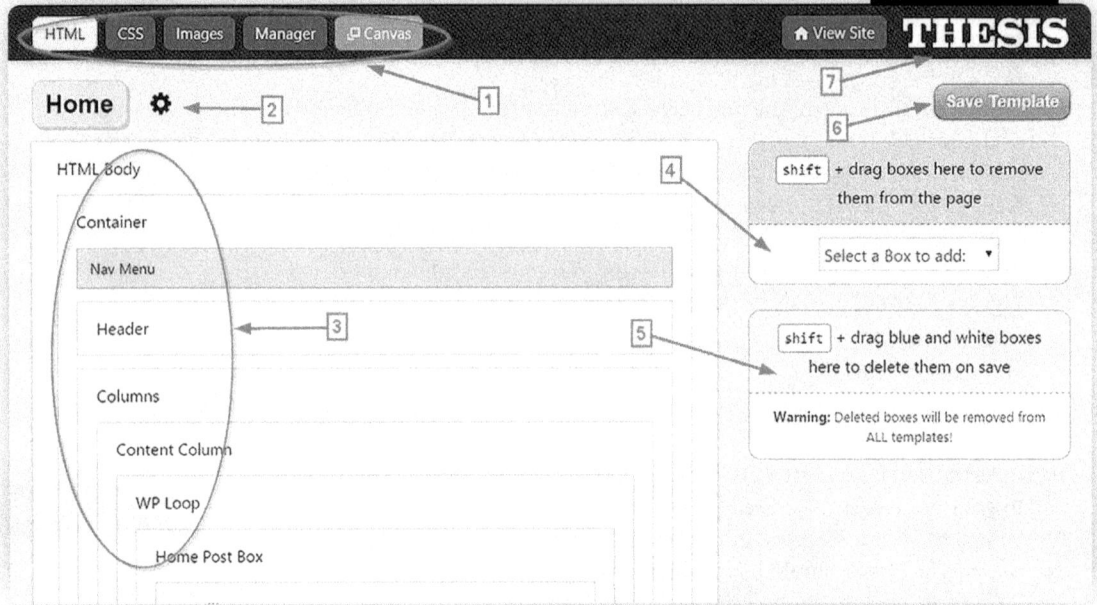

FIGURE 3.19

Skin Editor

The skin editor is the heart of Thesis. It is here where the design of your website can be meticu-lously controlled. The interface of the designer environment does take some getting used to and can be quite daunting at times. We will take you through it step-by-step so you can employ every aspect of it you want.

To start, open the skin editor by using **Thesis > Skin Editor** from the admin menu or from **Skin > Editor** on the top menu. You will be taken to a completely different design area and typi-cally to the *Home* template designer. Figure 3.19 shows this to you.

We have pointed out six of the major areas of interest. [1] is the menu bar where you switch between main areas of concern. You start in HTML mode and can switch to CSS editing mode, image management mode, manager control mode, or canvas mode. Each mode will be discussed in greater detail later in this chapter.

Starting in HTML mode, note these areas: [2] the page or template control button. Here you can switch between page templates; many are preset for you based on the currently active skin. Also note the gear icon beside this button, it triggers a pop-up dialog window in which you can control some page wide settings, but more on that later. There is the layout control area of the page template [3], here you can manage the sequence of what is displayed on your template. Will the Nav Menu be displayed first or image banner, and so on. [4] is the control area where you select additional boxes, activate these boxes, name them, control their settings, and place them within the template. The area below this [5] is where you can place boxes you do not want anymore. Be careful here, as they are deleted permanently from all templates when you save your work. Saving your work is done by clicking the **Save Template** [6] button. To return to the WordPress admin area simply click on the **Thesis** [7] area in the top right.

Back to the *Home* button [2], if you click this an overlay box is displayed showing all the page templates the current skin comes prepackaged with (see Figure 3.20).

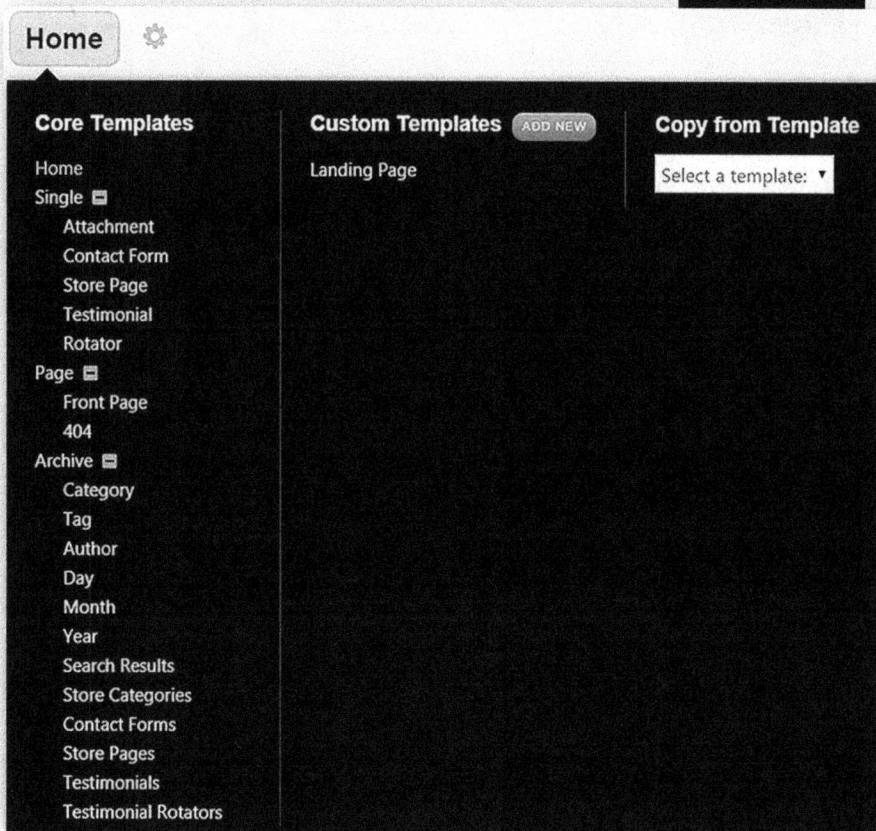

FIGURE 3.20

The major categories here (on the left of the list) are *Home*, *Single*, *Page*, and *Archive*. Notice also under the *Page* item are two other templates called *Front Page* and *404*.

Front Page *is the template page you would use if you have chosen to use a different page for your* home *landing page other than listing your latest blog posts. See* **Settings > Reading**. Home *is the page template connected to the listing of your latest list of blog posts. This can be confusing to keep straight.*

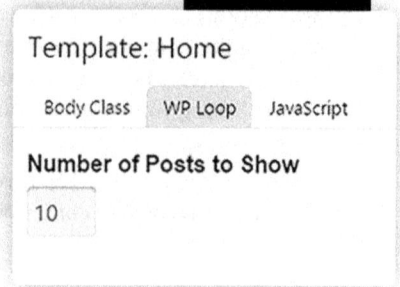

FIGURE 3.21

Template: Home

Body Class   WP Loop   JavaScript

Number of Posts to Show

10

The *Single* template is what is shown when a single blog post is displayed. The *Page* template is for displaying website pages other than the optional *Front Page* and *404* page templates. The archive collection of templates is used for specific topic pages. For example, if you had an ecommerce website then you would likely use the *Store* collection of template pages to manage layout and display of your inventory items.

To the right of this list are two other columns. The rightmost is where you would copy an existing template and reuse most of its features for a slightly different purpose. For example, if you did not like the offered 404 page layout, you could copy it, rename it, change it, and use the changed template on your site. Taking this example to fruition: you would name the new 404 template to something like *New404*. This would then appear on the middle column called *Custom Templates*. You would then create a WordPress page called *404 page* and there you would set the template name to *New404*, the name you gave it in the Thesis skin editor–under the page's section titled *Thesis Skin Custom Template*. Then, under the Thesis top menu select **Site > 404 Page** and pick the **404 Page** page as the one to display in a 404 (page not found) situation.

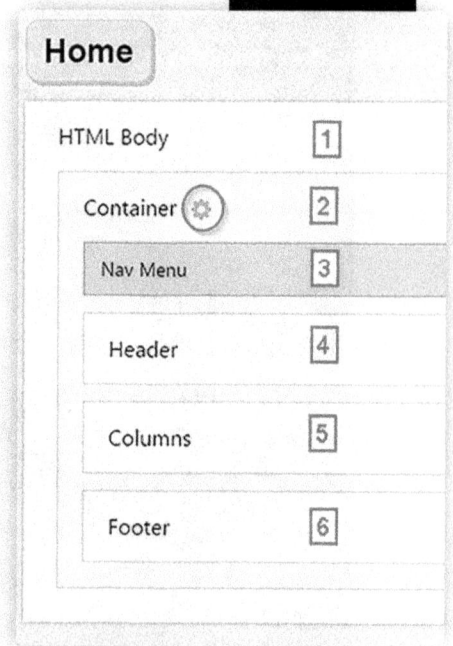

FIGURE 3.22

Home

HTML Body	1
Container ⚙	2
Nav Menu	3
Header	4
Columns	5
Footer	6

Getting back to the skin editor, if you click on the gear icon beside *Home* you will see the overlay shown in Figure 3.21 with the *WP Loop* tab selected.

As mentioned earlier, here you can set some values for the overall page in question. This works the same way for all templates, the only difference would be for pages which loop through content like a list of posts. The tags on this page control the body class name used on the template, if you want to change the value for some reason. You can change the number of posts to show on the looping control (default is 10) and use JavaScript Control. JavaScript Control allows you to select certain libraries to add to the templates and it also allows you to bring in custom scripts if you want to use any not in the predefined list.

In all of the skin editor templates you will see bands or rows of design. These rows can contain other rows and those rows can contain still more rows, and so on. As shown in Figure 3.22 with all the rows collapsed except for the top level, you can see the HTML body [1] row contains all the other rows and the container row [2] inside it possesses rows [3] to [6]. *HTML Body* is the overall "manager" of the content in this template.

Note all the rows have their own gear icons as well. This allows for granular control on the row settings. Take some time to explore these for yourself as most of them have similar values which can be set.

Expanding the header row [4] you will see two more rows colored purple (default) entitled *Site Title* and *Site Tagline*. The colors are significant, in that they indicate what type of row each one is. Purple in this case, signifies areas or data native to WordPress. Other colors are soft yellow and soft blue. These signify container elements and content boxes, respectively. There are also soft red rows which are generally special controlling items added into the skin by Thesis. These colors are loosely assigned but are in place to help you with designing the elements within each row. Practice and experience are needed here to get proficient with row content and design, but once you get the hang of it you can customize your site without editing templates.

Note some elements will be shown here as a default but they can be disabled from being displayed from the control area on the Skin Content page under the display options section.

To move the rows around within their container simply mouse drag and drop them to where you want them to be. When you have the row "in hand" it will begin to float and its background will turn yellow. In our case of the *Header* we can move the site title and tagline rows within the named container, but we can't move it outside the container via this method. To do that, you have to hold down the shift button and then drag-and-drop the element rows you want to relocate. For example, you could move the site title to the *Container* level via this method.

It is important to note these design features are quite powerful, so be sure to have a playpen or practice site area where you can experiment with your design ideas. This should be the development version of your site as we discussed in *Chapter 1* There is so much "rope" available here you need to be careful not to "hang yourself". Also remember these design changes are on a template by template basis. So if you make a significant change, like moving

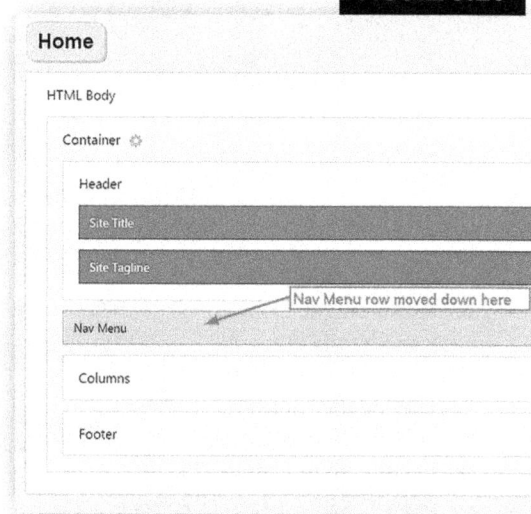

FIGURE 3.23

Home

HTML Body

Container

Header

Site Title

Site Tagline

Nav Menu row moved down here

Nav Menu

Columns

Footer

the location of the Nav menu, you will have to repeat those changes on all the other templates on your site if you want the change to be uniform (page, single, front page, 404, and so on).

Let's do a simple design change here to show you how it's done. We want to move the Nav menu below the *Header* container effectively moving the menu to display below the site title and tagline. Since the Nav menu row is on the same "level" as the header row we can simply drag-and-drop it to below the header as shown in Figure 3.23.

Save the template and then refresh your public facing content. It should look like Figure 3.24. Notice if you have selected the *Sample Page* or *Contact Us* menu items their design has not been altered. Move the Nav menu back to its original location and re-save your template.

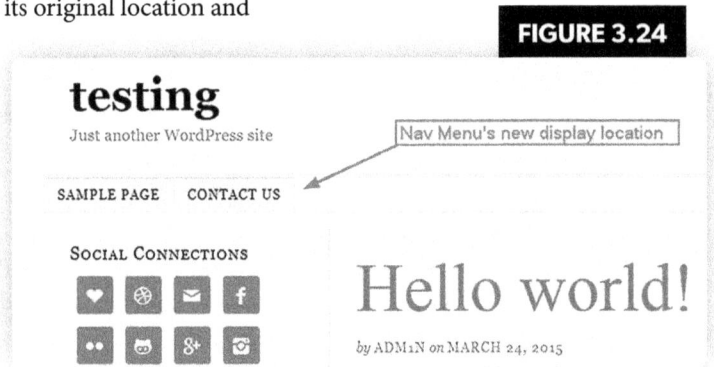

FIGURE 3.24

If you look at *Chapter 4* you will see we recommended adding in a plugin called *Open Hook*. Read that section if you have not already and then come back here. What the open box plugin allows you to do is to insert raw HTML, text, or even PHP code into your template. Another form of box you can use is called *text box*. This is a more controlled box where you can enter HTML or text only, no PHP code is allowed so it is a little more secure. Let's add a new text box with a welcome message on our *Home* template. This process will be the same for any rows or containers you add to a template. The only differences will be what type of row or container you will be adding. On the top right side of the template editor expand the drop-down list titled *Select a Box to add*. You will see a lengthy list of options. Pick the *Text Box* option and click **Add Box**.

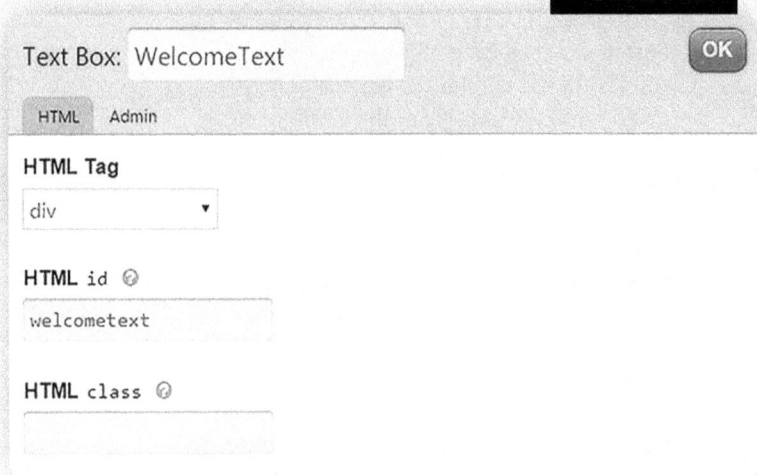

FIGURE 3.25

If you pick a wrong box at any time, simply shift and drag and drop the item into the grey area above the list to remove it from your work area.

Next, you should give the text box a unique name so you can identify it in your design. Click on the gear icon beside the name and you will see an overlay like the one shown in Figure 3.25.

FIGURE 3.26

Home

HTML Body

Container

Nav Menu

WelcomeText ⚙

Header

Site Title

Site Tagline

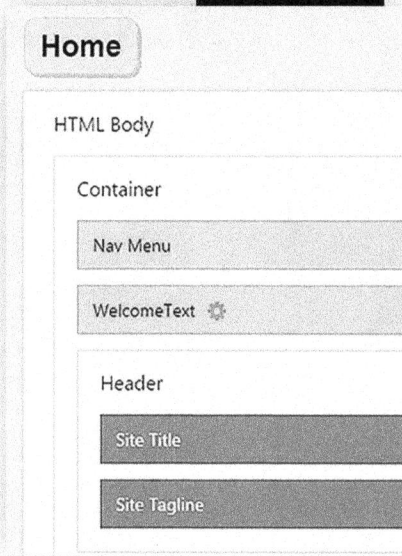

Here we have named the box *WelcomeText* and assigned an HTML CSS ID attribute to it with the value of `welcometext`. Also note this box will be controlled in the generated HTML with div tags (HTML Tag). You will see the name of this box then updated in the display. Now shift and drag and drop this box over to the template design area and set it between the Nav menu and the *Header* container. Just drop it in the *Container* area then drag-and-drop it to the correct location. Figure 3.26 shows this box properly placed. Save your design changes.

Next, we have to add some content to this newly created box. Close the skin editor by clicking on Thesis in the top right and open the **Skin > Content** page. You will see a new entry on the link list called *WelcomeText*. Click on it to open the editor. Figure 3.27 shows this editor with the welcome text and HTML entered into it.

Note the text box at the bottom of Figure 3.27 for controls the wrapping of text within the editor and how it is displayed on the public website.

Add this text yourself or some content of your own choosing and click on *Save Options* to save your work. Take a look at your public facing home page; it should look like Figure 3.28.

FIGURE 3.27

WelcomeText Options

Text/HTML ⊘

```
<br/>
<h2 style="color: orange;">
Welcome to our testing website,
we hope that you have <strong>fun</strong> looking around
and that you come back often.</h2>
```

☐ disable automatic <p> tags for this Text Box

FIGURE 3.28

SAMPLE PAGE   CONTACT US

Welcome to our testing website, we hope that you have fun looking around and that you come back often.

testing

Just another WordPress site

SOCIAL CONNECTIONS

♥ ⊕ ✉ f

Hello

One last section to cover in the skin editor is how to control the looping content of the display of blog posts. Go back into the skin editor and make sure you are on the *Home* template. Expand all the *Columns* rows if they are not already expanded. You should see what Figure 3.29 is showing.

Thesis pre-designs the layout of what is shown for blog posts, but you can certainly adjust it to your own needs. If you match the image number box in Figure 3.29 and 3.30 you will see the correlation between the rows showing post data. [1] is the placement of the author avatar, [2] the post headline, [3] the location of the post's author name and the date it was published, and so on. These can be rearranged as desired, of course. Keeping in mind the actual display of this information controlled in the **Skin > Content** area. Note the grey areas which have been circled in Figure 3.29. The first one is the separator between what is being displayed in the template and what other information is available to be displayed and the second is a way to hide the display of this offering if you want to have your design area less cluttered.

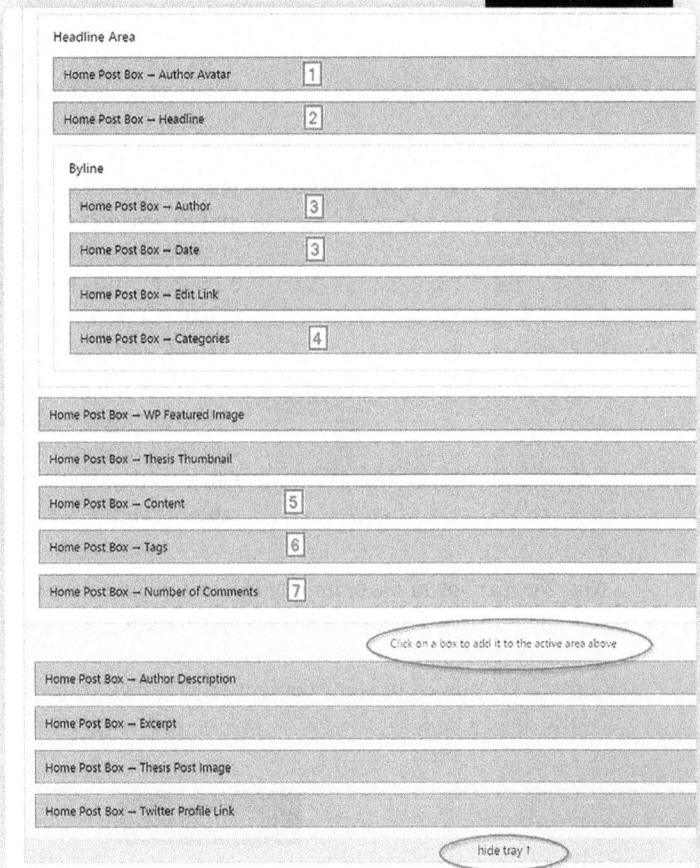

FIGURE 3.29

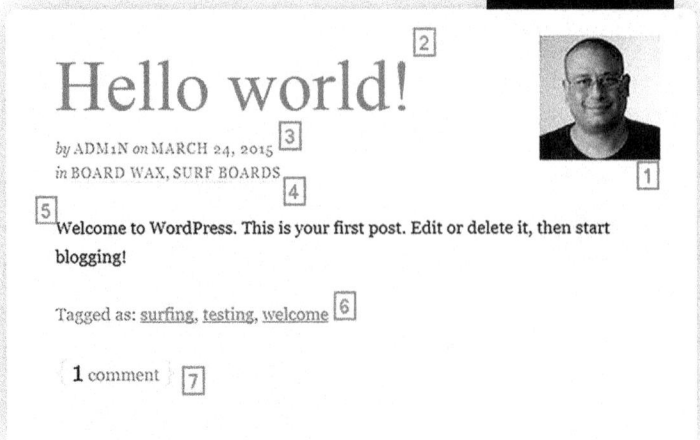

FIGURE 3.30

Custom Templates

Although Thesis has many pre-built templates for use in the skin editor, the developers realize there may be reasons for you to want to venture out on your own in the template design arena. Enter *Custom Templates* which can be accessed from within the skin editor by clicking on the current template button (usually *Home*). See Figure 3.20 for a menu reference. Under the Custom Template area, you can select existing custom templates which may have been created before or you can add new ones by clicking on the blue **Add New** button. When you click this blue button you are asked to name the new template. Be careful in your naming since you can give this template the same name as existing core templates or even repeat the names of existing Custom Templates. It is therefore recommended that you give the new template a unique name. If you make a naming mistake or you simply want to delete a template, you can click on the red "X" (while hovering on its name) on the right side of all the templates which are not in focus (not currently being edited).

Once you name and create a new template you will be switched to edit mode for the new template. Figure 3.31 shows the editor with a new empty custom template entitled *New Custom Template*.

All you are given by default upon template creation is a starting HTML body container. Everything else is a blank canvas. Remember you have all the box containers on the right side of the design surface at your disposal and you can create something

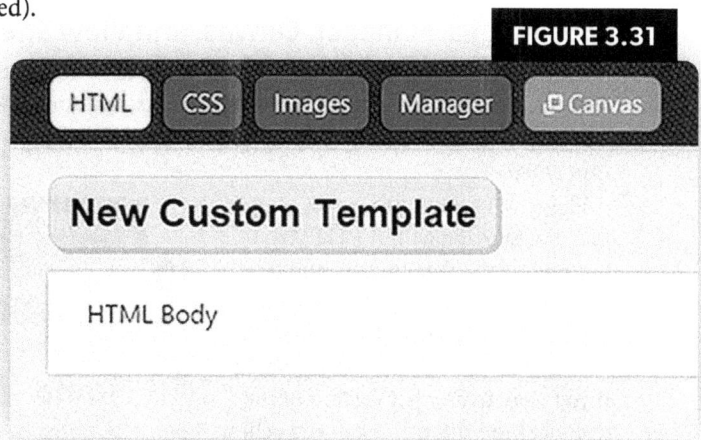

FIGURE 3.31

absolutely unique if so desired. If you get into trouble you can always delete the template and start over. So be sure to save often and add the new template to a dummy page (select the template name in the *Thesis Skin Custom Template* section of the page design area) to see what your creation looks like as you build it step-by-step.

Copying Templates

Alternately, if you have a template you want to use and you only want to adjust a small portion of it then copying an existing template will save you a lot of design time. Still under the design menu on the right side you can select an existing template to copy. **Be careful though**, since what you are doing is actually replacing the template currently in focus. This is not entirely intuitive to the designer (you), so be sure to create a new template first (following the steps above), *New Custom Template* is our example, and with it in focus, copy from the original *Home template*. See Figure 3.32 for the highlights.

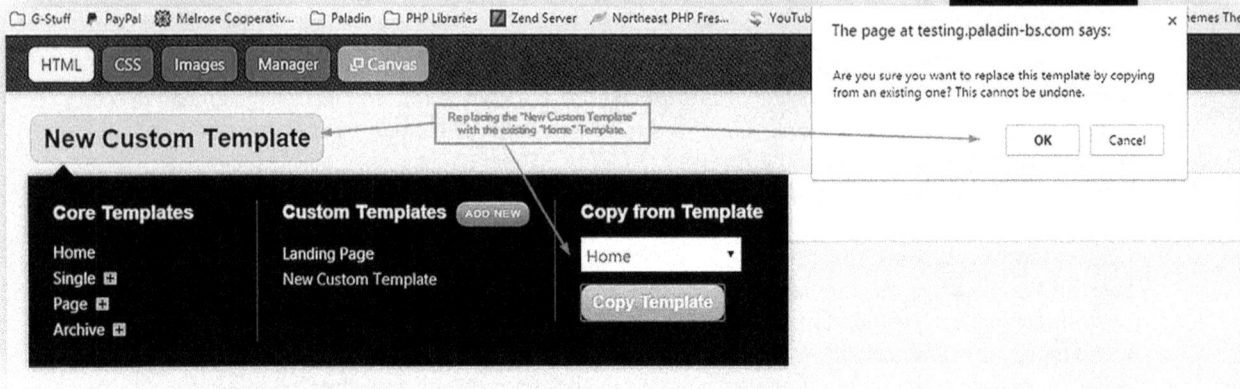

FIGURE 3.32

CSS, Images, Manager, Canvas, and View Site Buttons

In the Skin Editor at the top of the design area you will see a collection of buttons respectively named: *HTML, CSS, Images, Manager, Canvas*, and further to the right, *View Site*. We'll talk about these sections of the skin editor in this one section as they are all basic administration functions.

Figure 3.33 shows these command buttons. Starting with the HTML button it is the default view you land in when you start the Skin Editor. It is actually the button you would click on to return to the Template design area if you were in another section of the overall Skin Editor. It is colored yellow to signify it is the command function that currently has focus.

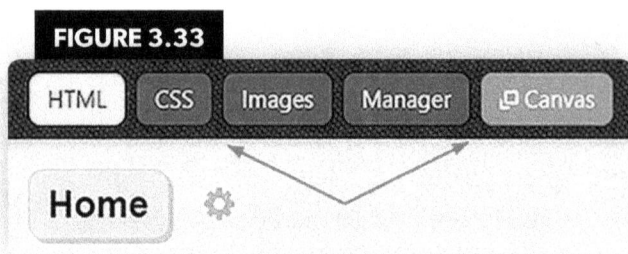

FIGURE 3.33

The CSS button takes you into the CSS area for the current overall active skin. Remember Thesis has many Skins it can use: Classic Responsive, Promo, etc. If you want to alter the CSS for any of these skins, then you can look at the settings of the CSS here and make changes if you want to; keeping in mind each Skin has its own unique CSS content. You will notice there are two tabs on the CSS editor: Skin CSS and Editor CSS. The main CSS work of the active skin will be within the Skin CSS tab area. Staying in the Skin CSS tab, it is recommended however, you adjust your CSS in the Custom CSS area (see next section in this chapter) rather than in this CSS area as it is "cleaner" to make the changes there as this CSS area is more technically directly involved with the skin itself. The one exception here is the use of CSS variables. On the right side of the CSS editor you will see a listing of the existing variables Thesis has already created as part of the currently active skin. You can additionally create your own variables by clicking on the blue **Create Variable** button. This variable creation and editing dialog is shown in Figure 3.34 where we have clicked on the existing variable named $font.

One of many new features in version 2.2 is the ability to change the CSS of WordPress' Post editor from within the Editor CSS tab here in the Skin Editor. As a quick example, let's change the default color of the H2 heading within the editor to red. While on the Editor CSS tab enter the following CSS and save your changes:

FIGURE 3.34

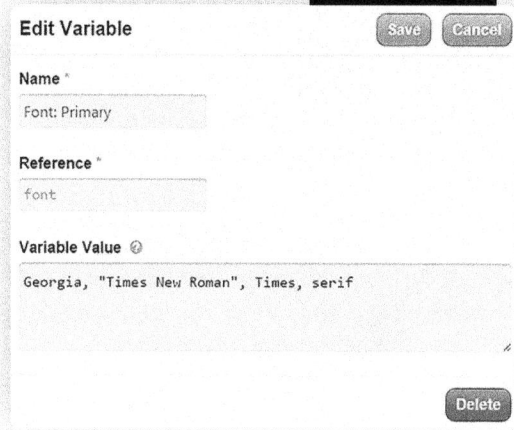

```
h2 {
    color: red ;
}
```

Next, go to any WordPress post entry you have on your site, we will use the simple *Hello World* post that is auto-generated for you when WordPress is initially installed. Switch the editor view to Text and add the following HTML:

```
<h2>this is a test</h2>
```

If you switch back to the visual display you should see something like that shown in Figure 3.35.

This is a neat feature to employee if you are creating a website heavily dependent on Blog entries, however these CSS changes will also affect WordPress pages within your site.

FIGURE 3.35

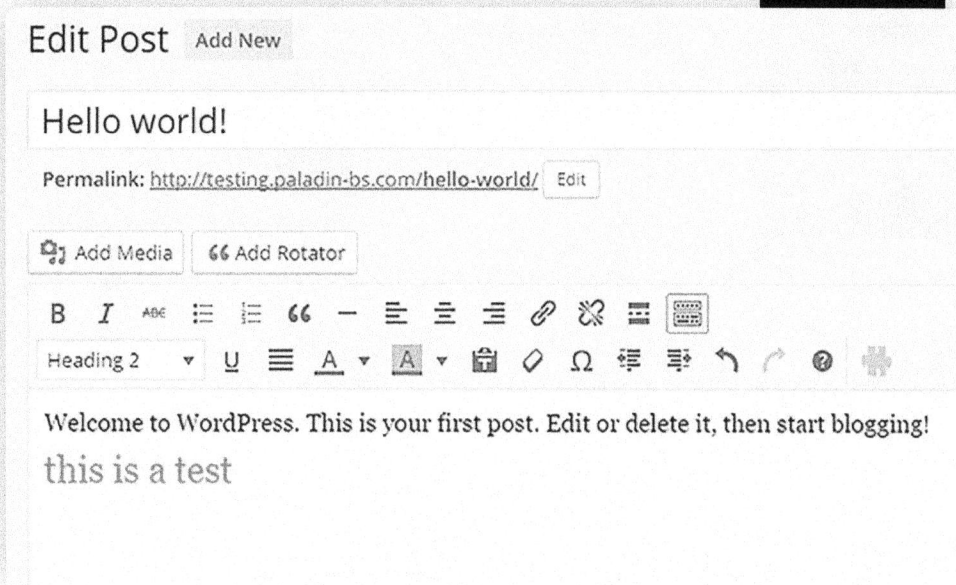

The **Images** button is an alternate way to add media to your site. In this context it is an area where you would upload images specific to your active skin. These images would not be available if you changed skins. This also differs from the site wide media library in that it does not upload the files to folders created for each month as the media library does. This allows for more direct identification of image files for use in your CSS or in your skin content and design areas. The drawback to uploading images here is you would have to either remember or copy the path to the image file itself in order to use it elsewhere on your site—in a page or a post, for example. The risk here is you may end up bloating your server with multiple copies of image files but a good designer would (should) know better! Keep in mind the images uploaded here are intended to be used within the Thesis areas of skin design and template use rather than as a site wide resource. Standard web friendly file formats are sufficient here: JPEG or PNG files. Figure 3.36 shows an image of a lighthouse (JPEG file) having been added to the Skin images library.

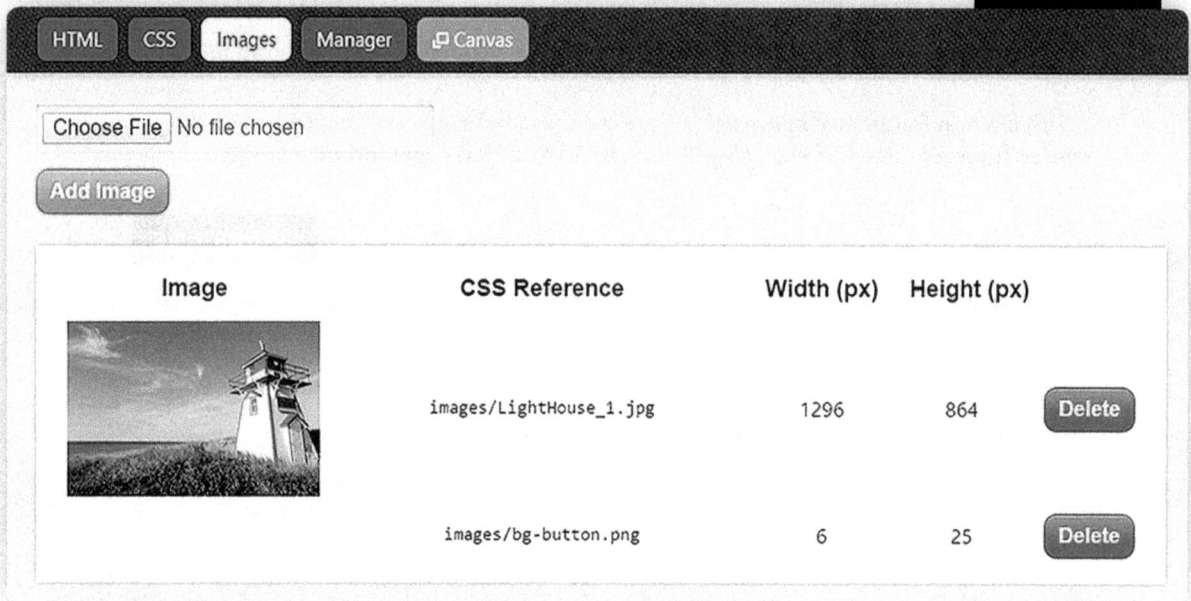

FIGURE 3.36

The **Manager** button is merely a way to export, back up, and conversely, import your skin. This is best used if you have made some specific skin changes like CSS changes, additions, or custom templates you want to replicate in another WordPress site. Keep in mind this is only for the currently active skin and does not act as a full system backup. Shown in Figure 3.37, you will also be shown any existing backups which have been made and are currently stored on the server. Additionally, there is an option to restore the skin to its default installation settings if you get into real issues with any of your alterations.

FIGURE 3.37

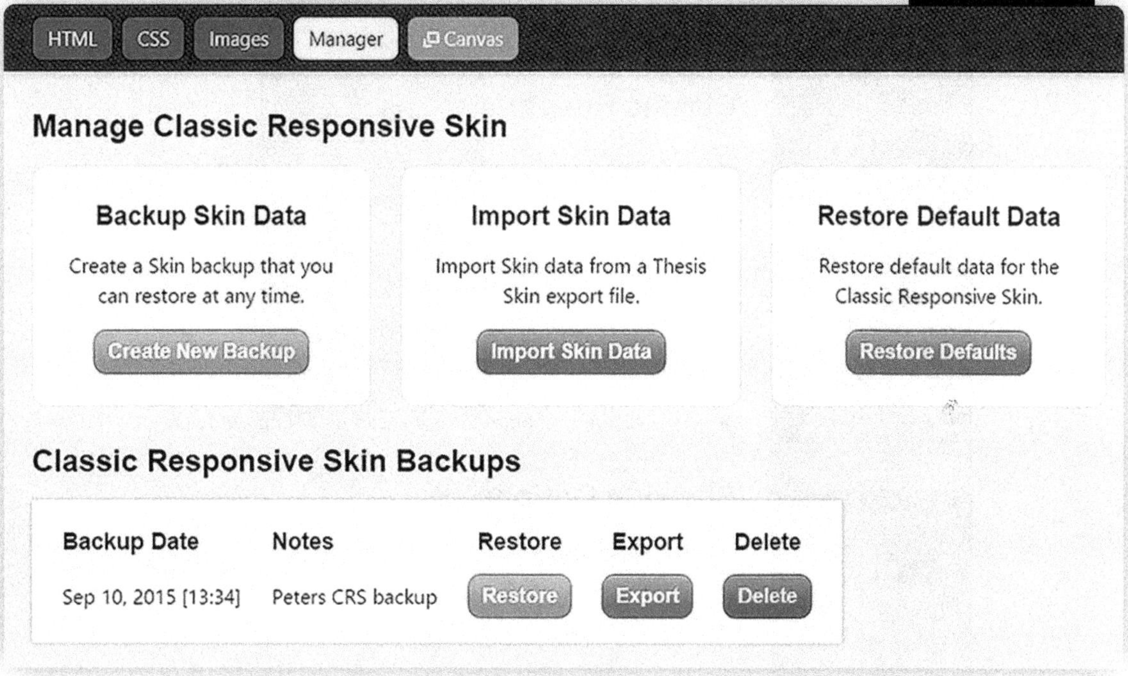

The **Canvas** and **View Site** buttons are almost identical in how they perform. The **Canvas** button shows you what your site looks like in the currently selected HTML template; it is displayed in a new window. This allows you to adjust the template and see what it will look like without having to open your public site in another browser. If you have two monitors you can make adjustments to the template on one screen, save the changes, and see the effect of those changes in the Canvas area immediately without having to refresh. It's a small victory, but can come in handy from time to time.

Conversely, the **View Site** button shows your site within the same browser tab.

Custom CSS

Thesis does not place any real limitations on you as a web designer. They have made a way for you to be very granular in your customization efforts. You can, as we saw in the previous section, adjust the layout and content on a per-page basis. Going even deeper, you can adjust the CSS for each class and ID in the individual Thesis skins. You can even create and name your own classes and IDs in the skin editor.

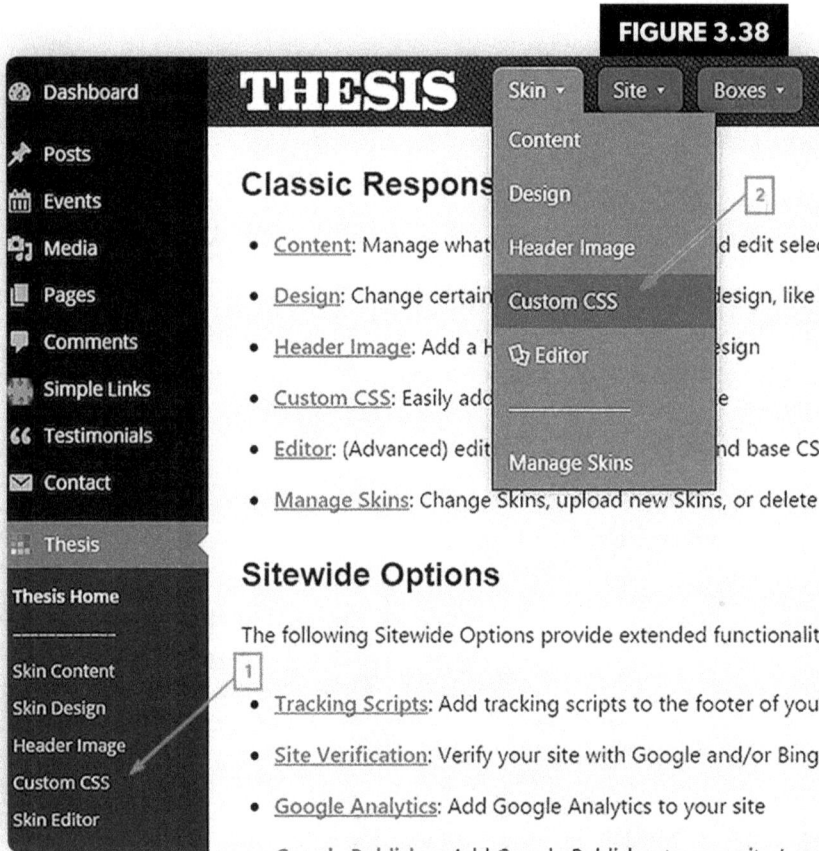

FIGURE 3.38

Let's start by looking at where you can perform this custom CSS work. There are two ways to get to the custom CSS editor shown in Figure 3.38. On the main admin menu select **Thesis > Custom CSS** [1] or on the thesis menu select **Skin > Custom CSS** [2]. Note that on the Thesis menu, the custom CSS option is under the skin menu; this implies each skin has its own custom CSS capability. If you have settings for a class by the name of post_content in one skin, you can have different settings for the same named class in another skin without conflict.

Upon opening the skin's Custom CSS editor you will be shown a basic text editor similar to that shown in Figure 3.39. If this is the first time you have opened this editor then, naturally, it would be blank. The editor will show line numbers and there is a page display (live preview) button as well. This page display button allows you to see the results of your CSS code before committing. And, there is always the save button on the far right of the page called **Save Custom CSS**.

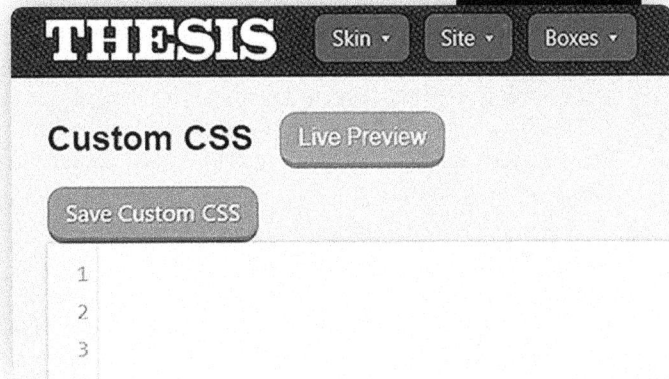
FIGURE 3.39

As with any markup you can get yourself into trouble if you don't format the CSS code properly or have it "well formed". If you are not getting the results you want, be sure to check the flow of your CSS code to ensure there are no missing semicolons or curly braces or that you don't have too many. If you have really complex CSS code you can use CSS Lint[1] to help with debugging it.

Also bear in mind many browsers have developer tools either built-in or which can be added on to them. You can inspect elements and CSS code via that mechanism as well.

If you want to use the variables which are created in the CSS editor in the Skin Editor (see previous section) then you can see a listing of these in this CSS editor by clicking on the plus (+) icon on the right side of the CSS code editor. A pop out list will display and you can see the listing of the existing variables. Clicking on any of the existing variable names will insert them into the code editor at the current location of the cursor. Also, if you hover over the variable name on the displayed list, it will give you more information about what each variable's values are.

When Custom CSS Fails to Save

On rare occasions you may find the save button on the custom CSS editor is disabled (broken). Clicking on it does nothing and you get no response from the editor bad or good. It has been my experience the cause of this behavior is that somehow the editor becomes disconnected from the database record storing the CSS code. Yes, that's correct, the CSS code (in Thesis at least) is stored in the database. The cause of this could be erroneous CSS code or a large volume of CSS code or both. The way to fix this is to first ensure your code is error free. Copy it to a local text editor if you can and test it on CSS Lint—if you can't copy it out of the Thesis admin editor you can do it later when you look at the CSS code in the database record. Next, you will need to have access to the database tables (you can use the Adminer MySQL interface plugin if needed).

[1]   CSS Lint: http://csslint.net

Locate the database table whose name ends in _options (usually it is named wp_options) and search for an entry with the following text at the end of its option name: _css_custom. If you're using the classic responsive skin the option name will be thesis_classic_r_css_custom. The option value of this table record is where the custom CSS is stored. You should ensure visually the first few lines of code match the code you have just moved to a text editor (if you could not move it to an editor before you can place it now, looking at the correct code) to have a confirmation that you're in the right place.

After you have your code fixed in a separate text editor, you can clean it out of the database record and save the record with its option value empty. This should trigger Thesis to start working again. You can then go back into the Thesis admin area and add your custom CSS code back in again. It is recommended to only add a few lines of "well formed" bug-free code and save it to make sure it's working and saving code content properly again. Next, try adding in all your CSS code and save it, if all is well, you can disconnect from your database to release those resources.

Manage Skins

Another great feature of Thesis is in how it manages and allows you to change the complete look and feel of your site with the use of skins. Whenever the mood hits you, you can change skins on the fly and your site will generally (depending on the specific template and CSS settings) react and reformat itself smoothly. There are two ways to access the skin management area. On the admin menu **Thesis > Manage Skins** [1] and on the inner menu **Skin >**

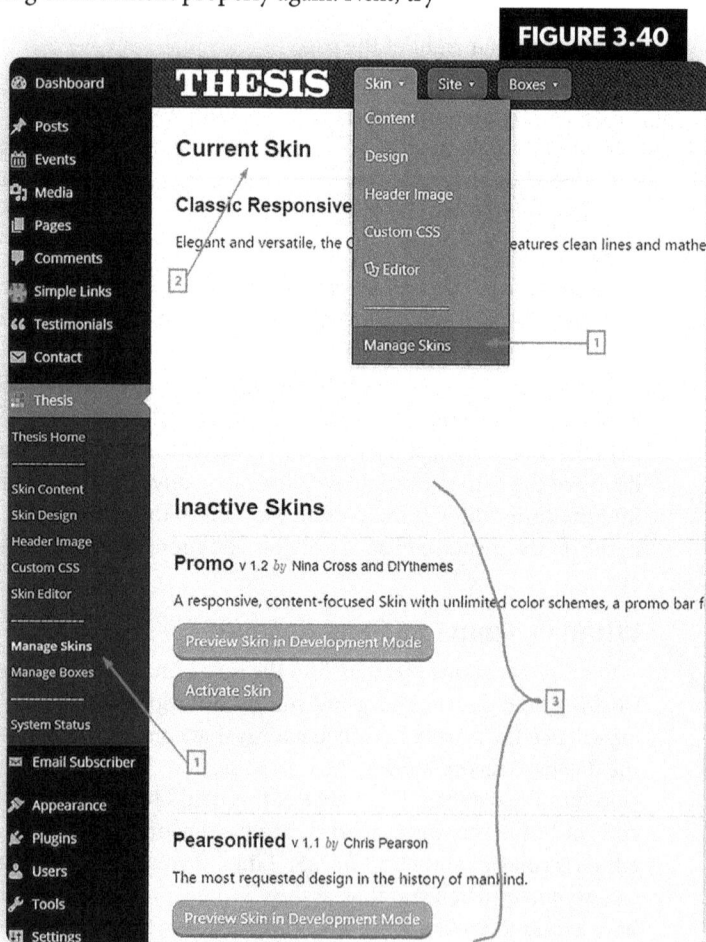

FIGURE 3.40

Manage Skins[1]. Both methods take you to the screen shown in Figure 3.40.

You will be shown the currently active skin [2], in our case *Classic Responsive* and then below that [3] you will be shown a listing of all the installed and available skins. If your site is in production you may want to click on the **Preview Skin in Development Mode** button to see what your site would look like without actually changing it. If you don't have those concerns simply click on the **Activate Skin** button next to the new skin you want to use and presto your site is changed. Of course if you don't want to have the slight overhead of keeping an inactive

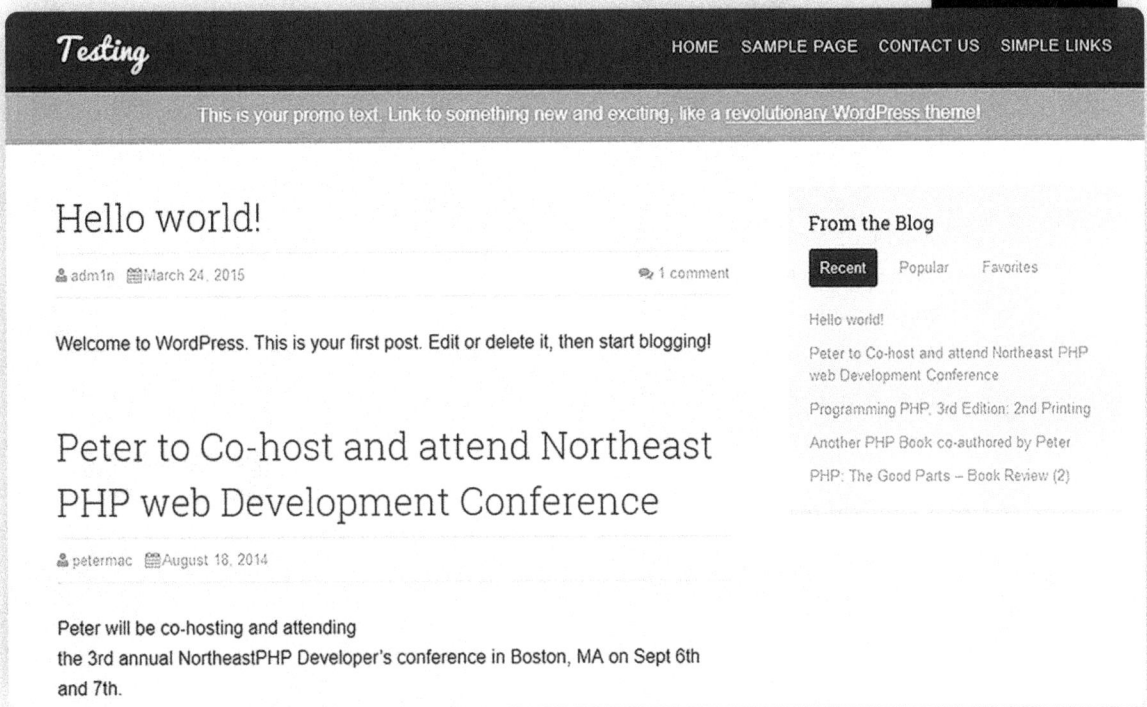

FIGURE 3.41

skin on your server you can always delete it by clicking the red **Delete Skin** button beside the skin in question. Figure 3.41 shows our testing site switched over to the *Promo* skin.

Manage Boxes

This is the area in Thesis where you can add tools to enhance and extend Thesis beyond how it was built. One such tool is called Open Box, which can be added on the Manage Boxes page–**Thesis** > **Manage Boxes** or **Boxes** > **Manage Boxes**. The page looks like the one shown in Figure 3.42 with the Open Box tool already installed.

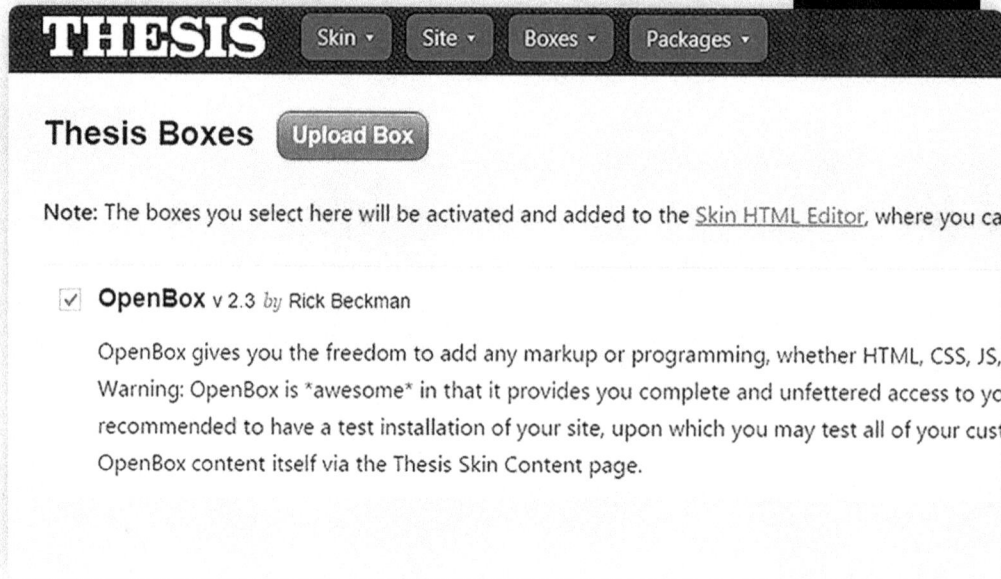

FIGURE 3.42

FIGURE 3.43

Once the box is added you can make use of it in either the Skin Editor (HTML section)–see Figure 3.40–or in the **Site > HTML Head** area depending on what the box tool was designed for.

This particular box (OpenBox) is also covered in Chapter 4 in the *OpenHook section*. The terms are synonymous. Also note you can turn these box tools on and off, or completely delete them from your website admin area if so desired. Since each box tool would have its own functionality we will not go any further on this subject here, so be sure to read up on the specific uses of any box you may want to employ on your sites before implementing them.

The Site Menu

Most of the items under the internal site menu lend themselves to helping you get your site noticed or tracked on the web. We will not be discussing all of these menu items in the following section, just the ones which make sense to highlight as they may be among the most useful. Anything you manage under this menu list will affect all your web pages on the entire site, not just the active skin.

Google Analytics Support

Thesis has the ability to include the JavaScript tracking code required for Google Analytics. As we mention earlier, Google Analytics is a free service you can register for. This tool tracks all your site visitor activity for you. From how many pages were viewed to what country your visitors came from. From the menu at the top of Thesis home select **Site > Google Analytics**. You will see a simple data entry page like Figure 3.44. Simply copy and paste in your tracking ID value and save your changes. Once verified, Google Analytics will begin actively tracking your sites analytics data.

However, in order to see the results of this data collection you always have to go to Google.

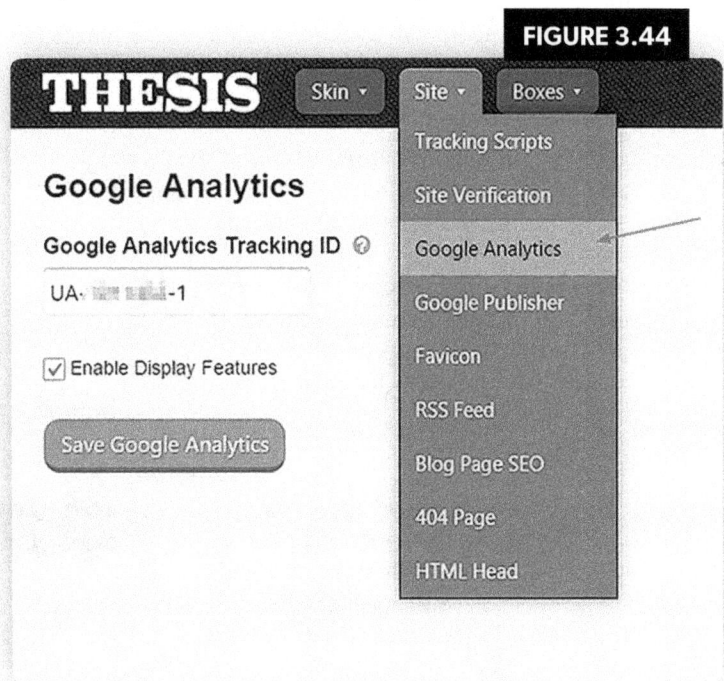

FIGURE 3.44

There is a more convenient plugin which shows the basic Google Analytics data to you within the WordPress admin area. The plugin is called *Google Analytics Dashboard for WP*. We cover it in detail in Chapter 5.

Google Authorship and Site Verification

This is a small additional item to Thesis. It allows for the addition of your Google+ information to be connected with your WordPress+Thesis site. This allows for "your author information to display in Google Search results". For what it's worth, you may want to consider making this kind of connection as it can help promote your site to show up more favorably in Google searches and to see errors or issues encountered when Google analyzes your site.

The next menu item under the internal Thesis *Site* menu is called *Site Verification*. This also lends itself to helping promote your site via Google and Bing verification methods. So if you really want to be found on the internet, you should employee these methods as well. Every little bit helps.

Tracking Scripts

The next menu item under the internal Thesis *Site* menu is called *Tracking Scripts*. It is a place where you can add any generic tracking scripts you want to include in your site. An example of this type of tracking code would be the default way Google Analytics tracked its information by generating script code for you to include on your site. You can use this if you decide to use another analytics service or if you want to track advertising results from social networks like Facebook or Twitter.

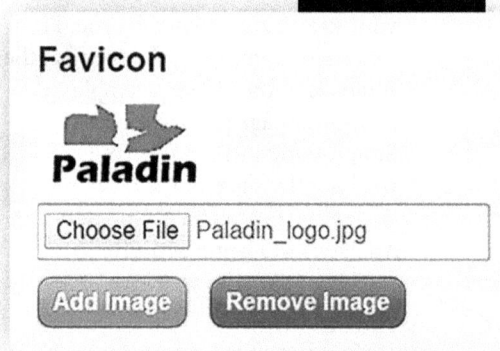

FIGURE 3.45

Favicon

Reached by **Site > Favicon**, the favicon area is simply a way to add this type of image to your web site. Figure 3.45 shows the management and upload page for selecting your image and uploading it to the site. The rest is done for you. Since the favicon area is generally small you should take some time to select an image that will look good where it will be used. See Figure 3.46 for a sample of where the favicon appears.

404 Page

Reached by **Site > 404 Page** it's the simple assignment area for a 404 page. A 404 page is the default page your site will display if a user requests a page which doesn't exist on your site and gets its name

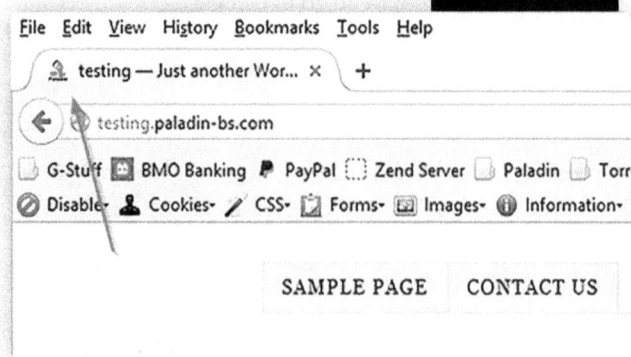

FIGURE 3.46

from the numeric status code used by web servers to tell a client a page cannot be found. It is an attempt at a graceful fail, so to speak. Here you can assign an existing page which will be displayed in that instance. Typically this page is used to instruct users to visit your home page, use your site search to find the page they requested, or provide an email address or link to your contact form to ask for further assistance. This can be further enhanced if you use the 404 page design area within the Skin Editor. Figure 3.47 shows this assignment area.

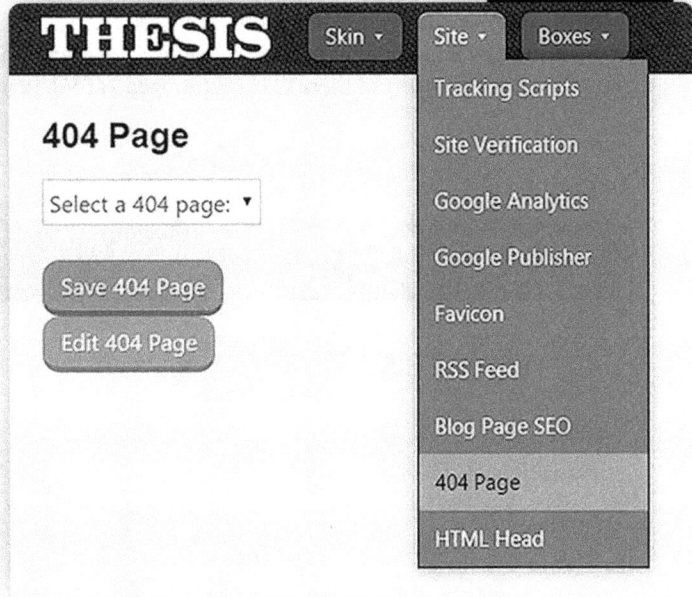

FIGURE 3.47

HTML Head

The last item on the Site menu is called *HTML Head*. Here you can better control anything you want to add into the head of all your web pages on the site you are building. Probably the best example here would be the addition of a unique font you want to use which is not used a typical website by default. We could add a Google font[2] by inserting the link tag with the specific font instructions that we want to use; see Figure 3.48.

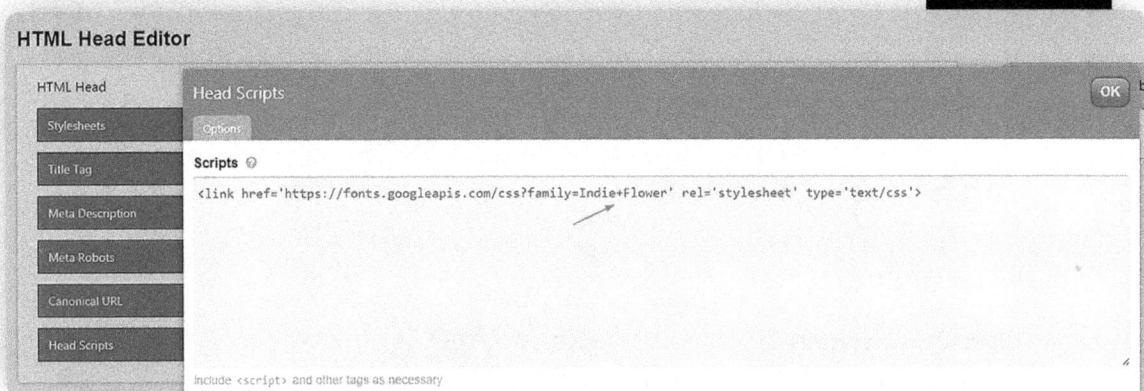

FIGURE 3.48

[2]   Google fonts: https://www.google.com/fonts

Once added, we can employ the font anywhere we want via the Custom CSS area. Here we are using it to change our H1, H2, H3, and A tags (see Figure 3.49). We see it in action on our website under a custom Skin content location called *WelcomeText* in Figure 3.50, and actually anywhere site wide which uses any of these CSS customized HTML tags.

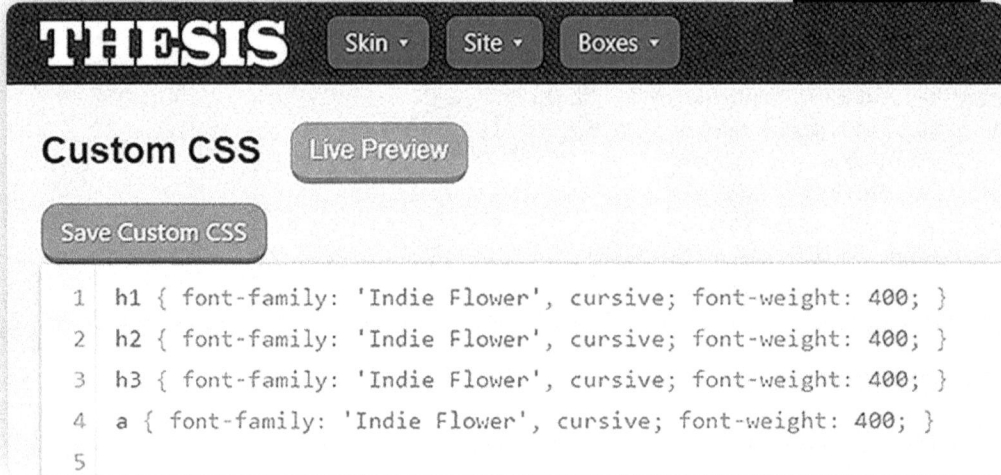

FIGURE 3.49

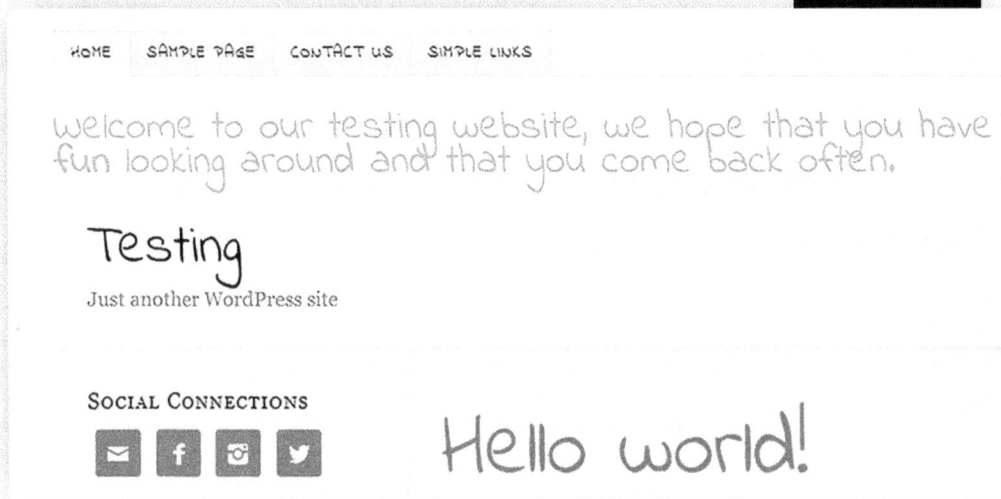

FIGURE 3.50

Chapter 4

The Best Plugins–Part 1
Simple Tasks

One of WordPress' strengths is the cornucopia of plugins available for free at *http://wordpress.org/plugins*. At the time of this writing there are 36,344 active plugins available to download and enhance your WordPress site. This is not even counting the many commercially available plugins which also exist. But—and this is a very big but—not all of these plugins are great or even applicable to a large audience of users. Some plugins have been created and released into the wild and their creators are never heard from again. Some are also created by their respective development teams and left to die on the vine, so to speak; never being updated, tweaked, maintained, improved, or debugged.

When you look at a plugin's details on the WordPress site, you will have the information needed to make an informed decision on whether or not you should trust it enough to try it out or even use it long term on your site. See Figure 4.1 for an example of this, where we are looking at the information page on the Akismet plugin.

FIGURE 4.1

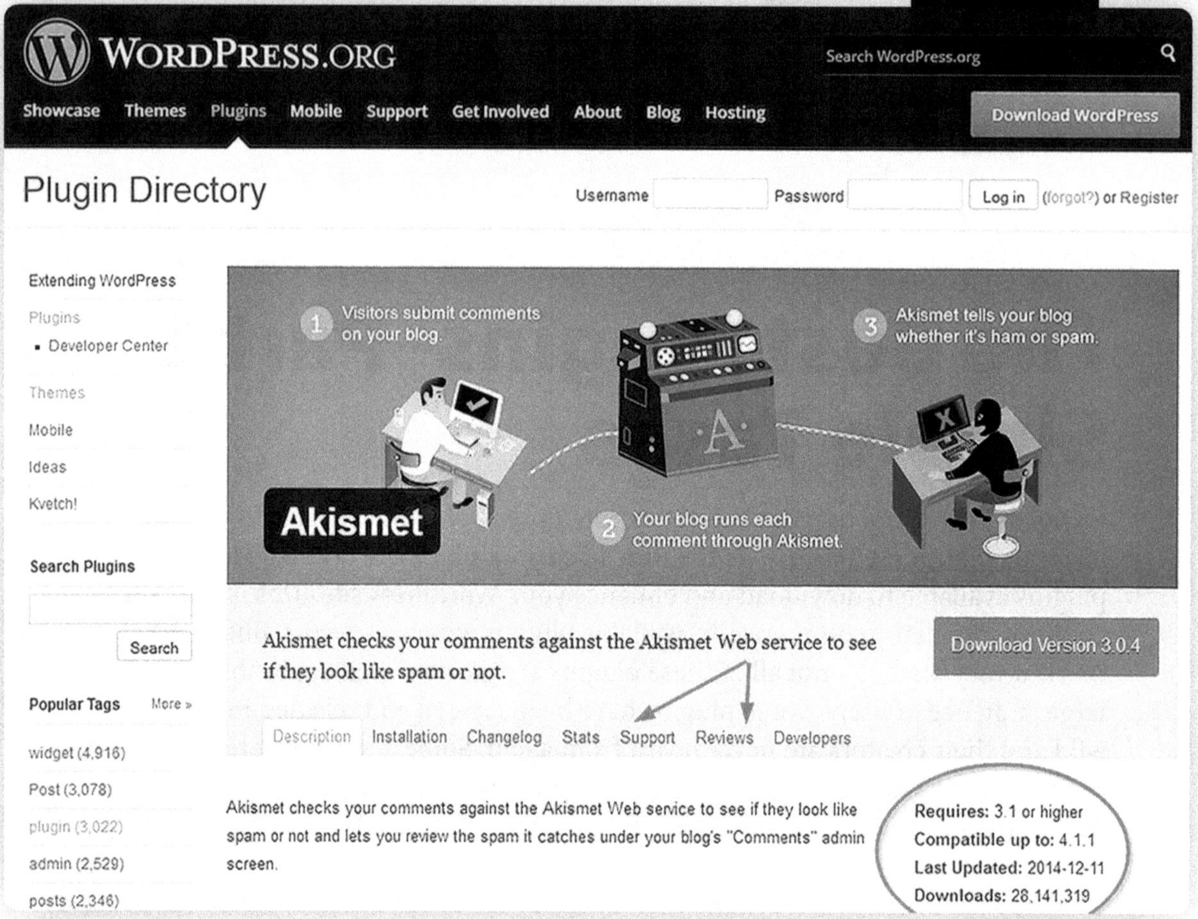

How should you evaluate a plugin? Besides the basic functionality of the plugin being of interest to what you want accomplished on your site (read the title and the description of the plugin), you will also want to take note of the compatibility of the plugin to the version of Word-Press you have installed. Additional key items to look for are:

1. The date of the last time the plugin was updated—although there are arguments a recent update does not necessarily mean the plugin is great. An older update could just mean a plugin has already gone through a number of updates and the developers are happy it's stable and therefore not in need of updates.

2. The number of downloads which implies the popularity and usefulness of the plugin.

3. Active *Support* and *Reviews* sections: look for feedback from users and from the community. Make note of how the plugin authors handle bug reports and feature requests.

These, all in concert with one another, lend credence to the plugin in question.

All of these factors however, do not guarantee a great plugin; therefore, we have selected a number of the best plugins we are aware of and will be describing them to you in the next two chapters. This chapter will cover the short-snappers: simple, usually one-task, plugins almost every site can benefit from implementing. The following chapter will cover larger multitask plugins like the WooComerce plugin for eCommerce.

Remember, these are just the plugins we use and have found to be stable, functional, and well supported. You may discover a similar plugin which suits your needs better. Full disclosure: we did not test all 36,000+ plugins!

A caution here: you should be conservative in your plugin use. The more plugins you install and employ could mean a higher overhead in demand for resources thus potentially reducing performance. And the more plugins you have, the more often you are likely to have to perform updates and be on the lookout for security vulnerabilities.

How to Install and Activate a Plugin

First, it is important to know how to install a plugin. There are a number of ways to install plugins on a WordPress site. In this section we will be discussing the two most popular ones: *seek + install* and *upload + install* (typically with a ZIP file). Both of these methods are completed within the administration area. Another method (not covered here) is to use (S)FTP to upload individual files directly to the filesystem and activate the plugin later, but that is typically only done in rare occasions—generally if you've developed a plugin yourself.

For simplicity, we will be installing all of our plugins in the next two chapters with one of these two common methods, primarily the seek + install method.

If you have any troubles with either of these two methods, check the WordPress codex for troubleshooting tips: https://codex.wordpress.org/Managing_Plugins#Troubleshooting

Through the Admin "Seek + Install" Method

In this method of plugin installation you simply access the **Plugins** > **Add New** menu item. This will bring up the add plugins page; see Figure 4.2.

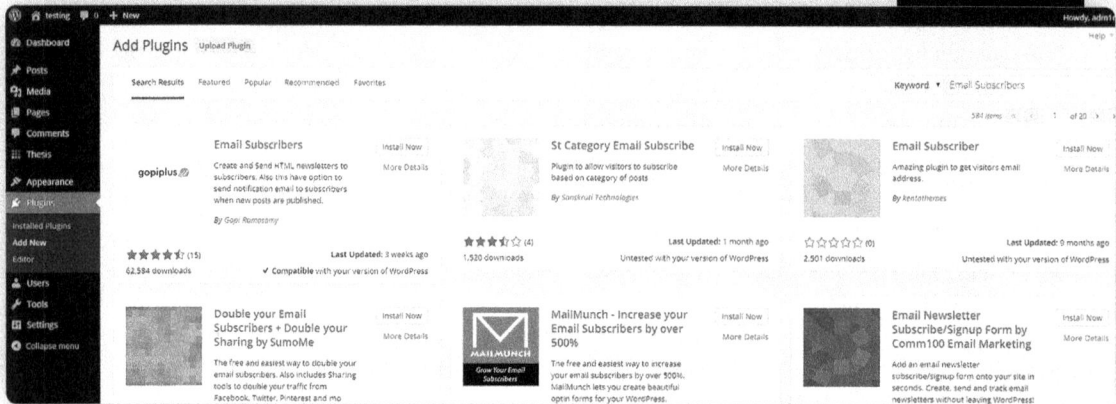

FIGURE 4.2

Here you are initially shown some featured plugins. Additionally, there are other menu items here you can use to see what's popular, recommended, and on your list of previously marked favorites (if you have already done this on WordPress.org). These four menu options are nice to use if you're in a shopping mood, or you just want to see what is trending from the WordPress community perspective. However, if you know what plugin you are after, and usually you do, just simply type in the name or topic of the plugin in the *Search plugins* text input at the top right of this page and press enter.

In our example, we searched for "Email Subscribers" which returned over 580 results! As you can guess, simple shopping for a plugin can potentially take hours. Once you find the plugin you're after, you can do further reconnaissance on it by clicking the *more details* link. This will open a pop-up window which will give you all the available details you might need on any particular plugin. Typical detail tabs are description, installation, screen shots, change logs, FAQ, and reviews.

If you are sure you've found the plugin you want, simply click on the **Install Now** button to start the installation process. You will get a confirmation screen, click **OK** to confirm your wishes, and the installation will commence (you may be asked for FTP credentials depending on how your WordPress site was initially installed). When completed, you will be given a choice to activate the plugin or return to the plugin installer, see Figure 4.3. If you choose the latter option, you are merely returned to the plugin installation page where you can repeat the process for more plugins if desired. Alternatively, if you click on the activate link, the plugin will be enabled and you will be taken to the *Installed Plugins* page which lists all the currently installed plugins for your WordPress site.

Once a plugin is activated, you should see some "proof" of this in the admin menu. Sometimes, as is true in this case, the plugin inserts its own menu item; however, some other plugins will show up under the *Tools* menu or the *Settings* menu. There is no hard and fast rule here, so if you don't see

FIGURE 4.3

Installing Plugin: Email Subscribers 2.7

Downloading install package from https://downloads.wordpress.org/plugin/email-subscribers.zip...

Unpacking the package...

Installing the plugin...

Successfully installed the plugin **Email Subscribers 2.7**.

Activate Plugin | Return to Plugin Installer

a newly created top-level menu item for your plugin you may have to hunt a little or refer to the plugin's documentation. Keep in mind some plugins are additions to the core functionality of WordPress and therefore may not have a menu item presence at all.

Through the "Upload + Install" Method

The other method, usually used with commercially available plugins (and themes), is to download a ZIP file and import it via the admin area. As is our example here, we will use the same plugin of *Email Subscribers*. After locating the desired plugin on WordPress.org, or at the website hosting the plugin, simply download and save it to your local system. Next, go to the same **Plugins** > **Add New** page in the admin area and this time click on the **Upload plugin** button at the top of the page. After this you will be presented with a file browsing dialog.

Locate the ZIP file you downloaded, select it, and then click the **Install Now** button shown in Figure 4.4.

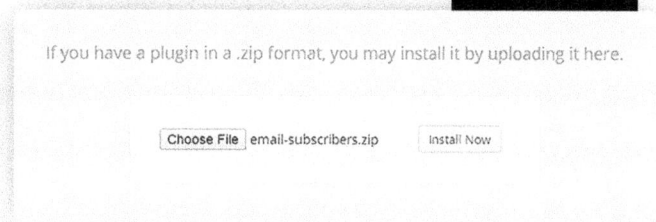

FIGURE 4.4

If you have a plugin in a .zip format, you may install it by uploading it here.

Choose File email-subscribers.zip   Install Now

All the remaining steps are the same as the previous method. You have to activate the plugin and then locate it somewhere in the admin menu system to make use of it. Let's look at some plugins most sites will find useful.

Akismet

Akismet[1] is a strange name for a plugin; you will see it as a default plugin on most WordPress installations and there is a good reason for this. Most blog sites allow readers to comment on posts, allowing them to reply with their own thoughts and ideas on the posted topic. However, there are ways spam can be added to these posts by web-bots and malicious software engines existing on the web. The spam these entities generate can quickly overload a site that is not doing a good job of protecting itself.

At the very least, even if you don't use this plugin, you should always have your comments

[1]   *Akismet: https://wordpress.org/plugins/akismet/*

set to *Pending* so you, or someone else, can review and approve any comments added to your blog before they are released to the public on the web. Under the **Settings > Discussions** menu option be sure you have *Comment must be manually approved* turned on. Also, be sure to review the other options available to you on this screen as they may also be helpful in limiting spam comments on your site.

Getting back to the plugin in question, Akismet is a hosted service which will scan any incoming comment submission and flag it as suspicious for you if it deems it to be so. The network of sites using Akismet helps the system learn to identify spam better. Once you activate the plugin, it will prompt you to provide an API key (see Figure 4.5). This key is used by the Akismet service for statistical purposes and they also have a commercial version for sale as well. A license is free—with limits—for personal blogs, but businesses, non-profits, schools, and other sites with significant traffic will need a paid license.

Actually, many plugins will offer a free version with some limitations placed on it like reduced features or reduced uses. Be sure to double check the license requirements on each plugin you use to ensure you are honoring their licensing requirements.

FIGURE 4.5

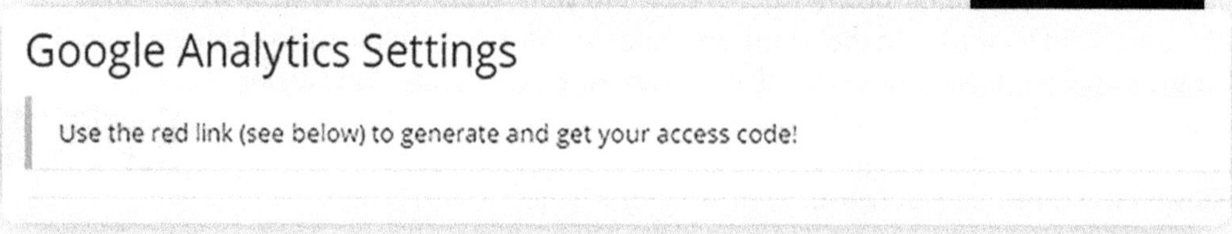

Google Analytics Settings

Use the red link (see below) to generate and get your access code!

Visit *http://www.akismet.com* for more details. Once you have the API key in place you have even more options available to you on how to deal with the spam this tool identifies for you. See Figure 4.6 for the available options.

FIGURE 4.6

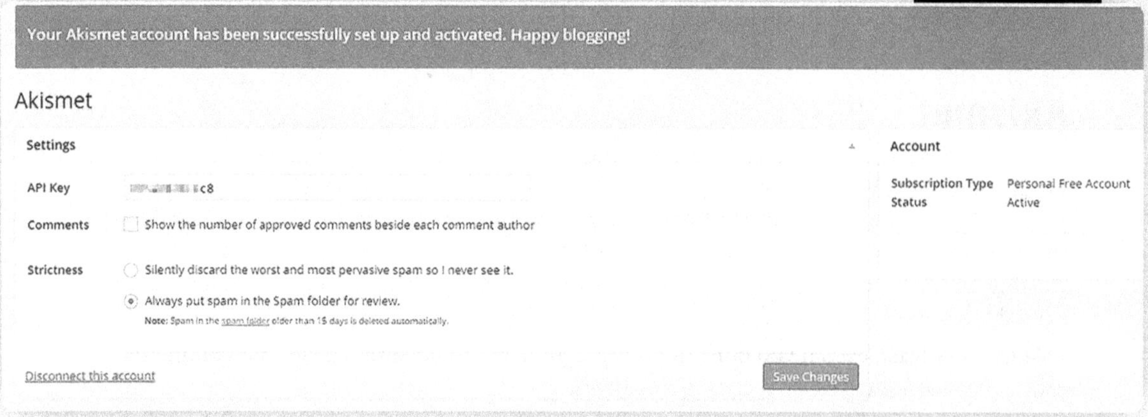

Your Akismet account has been successfully set up and activated. Happy blogging!

Akismet

			Account	
Settings				
API Key	⬛⬛⬛⬛ c8		Subscription Type	Personal Free Account
			Status	Active
Comments	☐ Show the number of approved comments beside each comment author			
Strictness	○ Silently discard the worst and most pervasive spam so I never see it.			
	◉ Always put spam in the Spam folder for review.			
	Note: Spam in the spam folder older than 15 days is deleted automatically.			
Disconnect this account			Save Changes	

You can always return to this settings page by way of the **Settings** > **Akismet** menu option.

Email Subscribers

One of the most common activities a blogger wants to do is to communicate with their readership on a regular basis. However, the proliferation of spam on the internet has made visitors cautious of giving out their email address. The site owner needs to be able to provide reassurance that if the visitor does indeed share their email address, the information will be in safe hands. The *Email Subscribers*[2] plugin allows for this type of safe and convenient mailing list management. There are two aspects to this plugin, the form and method of collecting subscription information and the admin side of managing the list of emails that have been collected. Figure 4.7 shows the installation of the *Email Subscribers* plugin.

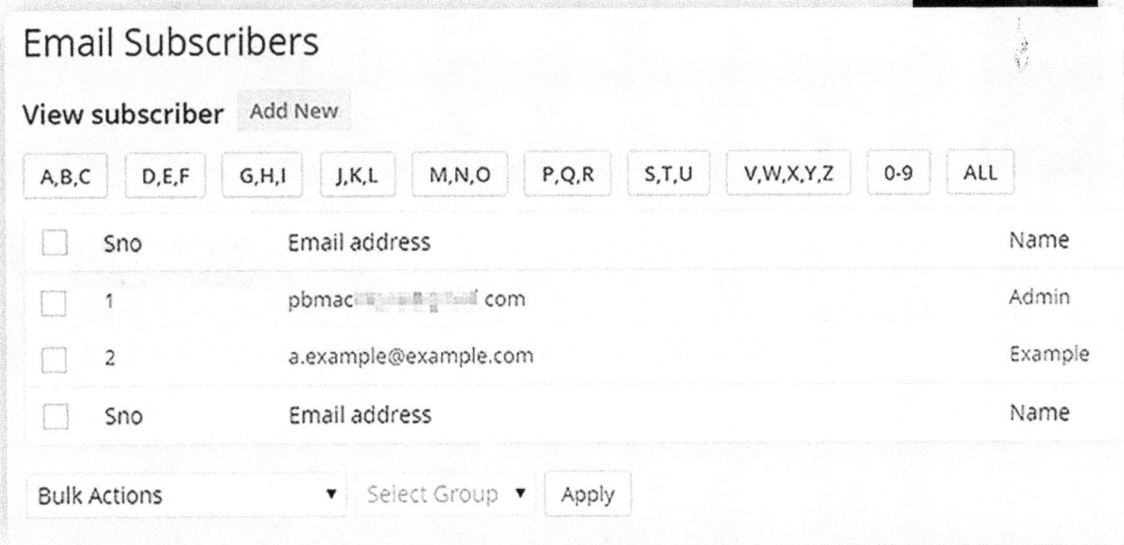

FIGURE 4.7

---

[2]   Email Subscribers: *https://wordpress.org/plugins/email-subscribers/*

Information Collection

In order to collect email information with this plugin you have to use its predefined form in a widget. The menu path **Appearance** > **Widgets** takes you to this area, see Figure 4.8. Simply drag-and-drop the widget control into the side bar location and make any detail adjustments you want. The resulting sidebar would look like the one shown in Figure 4.9.

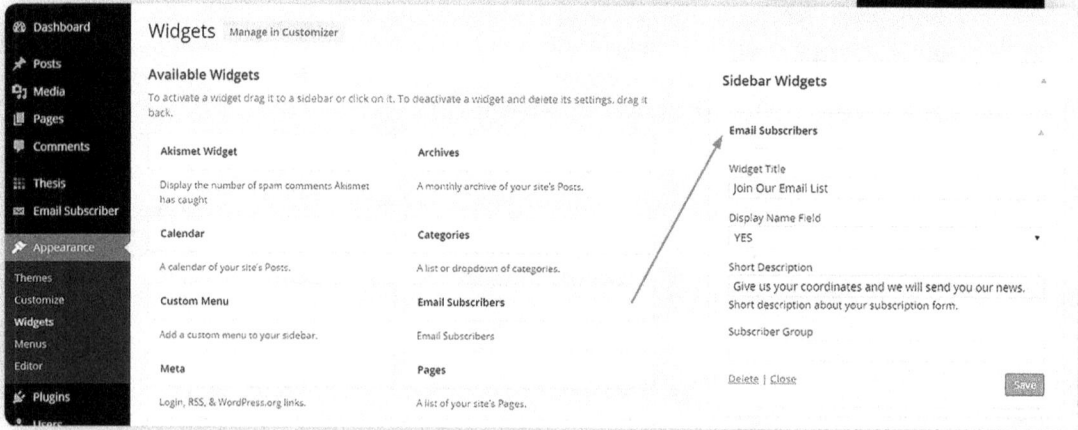

FIGURE 4.8

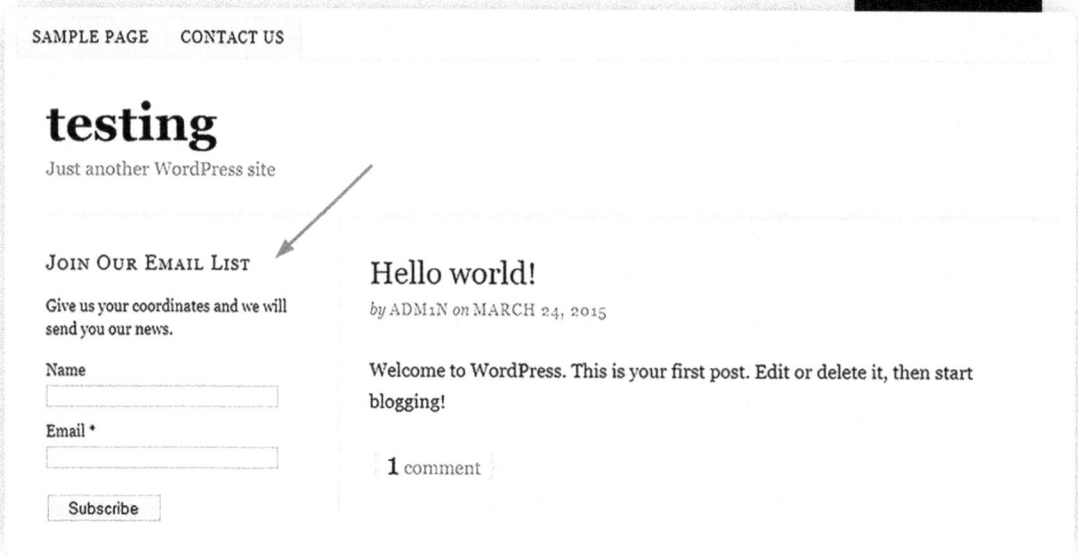

FIGURE 4.9

This form can also be used in regular site pages in the form of a short code. Merely enter the text similar to the following in your page to render the form for your visitors:

```
[email-subscribers namefield="YES" desc="" group="Public"].
```

The online help for this plugin is quite thorough and shows you many additional features. This can be seen in the last menu option under the email subscribers plugin menu called *Help and Info*.

List Management

The best feature of this plugin is it automatically sends an email to all of your subscribers whenever you create a new blog post on your site. You don't have to remember to send out an announcement, you only have to publish your post. There are many other options in this plugin which allow you to control the way your subscribers join the mailing list (single or double opt in), the content of the emails, the format of the emails (HTML or plain text), and so on. These can all be adjusted in the settings page.

Another nice feature of this plugin is the ability to build and send out email-based newsletters to your subscribers separately from your posts. If you have a special message you only want your subscribers to see and not have it posted generically on your website—this is the way to go.

> As alluded to earlier, you, the site owner, need to be calculated and conscientious about sending out too much content. Internet users generally do not want to be inundated with information, so try not to be "spammy" in the content and emails you produce. Also be sure to check if your hosting provider or email service has limits or bills you by the volume of email you send out.

Testimonial Rotator

Testimonial Rotator[3] is the next plugin we are going to look at and is one which typically shows content in a sidebar location via a widget. It displays multiple quotes or testimonials in a compact and limited space. This can be used to draw attention to special places or pages on your site or to list a series of testimonials of people who have sent you praise for your work or your accomplishments.

After installation and activation you will see a new menu item called testimonials at the main level of the *Admin* menu. Here is where you will create rotators. You can have multiple rotators for different contexts of your site. Simply enter the quotations, and fine tune the settings—you can set display time length, transition effect, the size of the attached image, and the transition speed between testimonials. You can even add the rotators directly into individual pages, as there is an **Add Rotator** button included in the text editor on both pages and posts. In Figure 4.10 you can see the listing of existing quotes which have been entered with the option to add more.

[3] *Testimonial Rotator: https://wordpress.org/plugins/testimonial-rotator/*

FIGURE 4.10

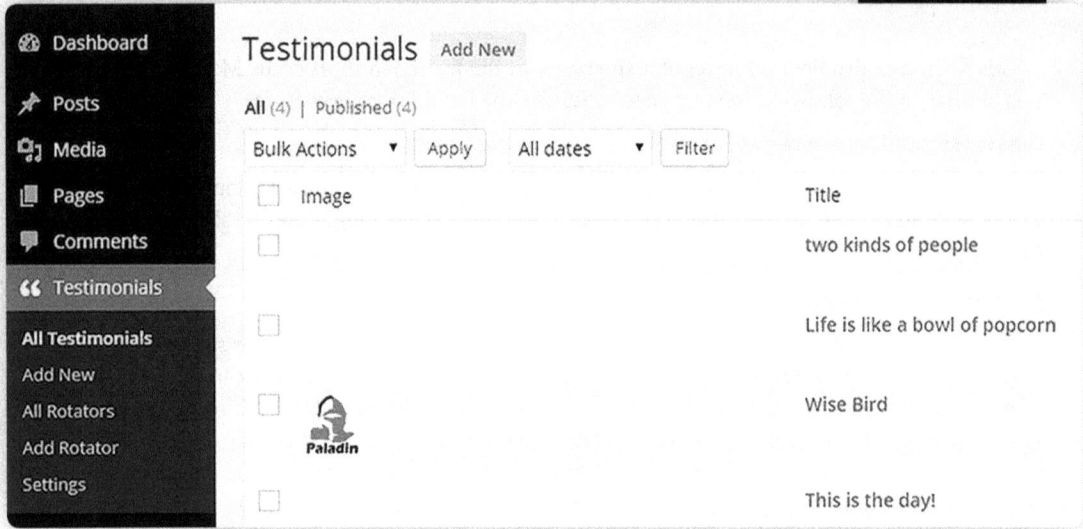

In Figure 4.11 we are editing an existing quote (we have rearranged the default layout here so your screen may look differently). In add / edit mode you can control some important options like giving a star rating, attaching the testimonial to different rotators (these have to be created beforehand), assigning an author (with option to add a link to a URL), and attaching an image to the testimonial. These are just a few of the many options and controls at your disposal.

FIGURE 4.11

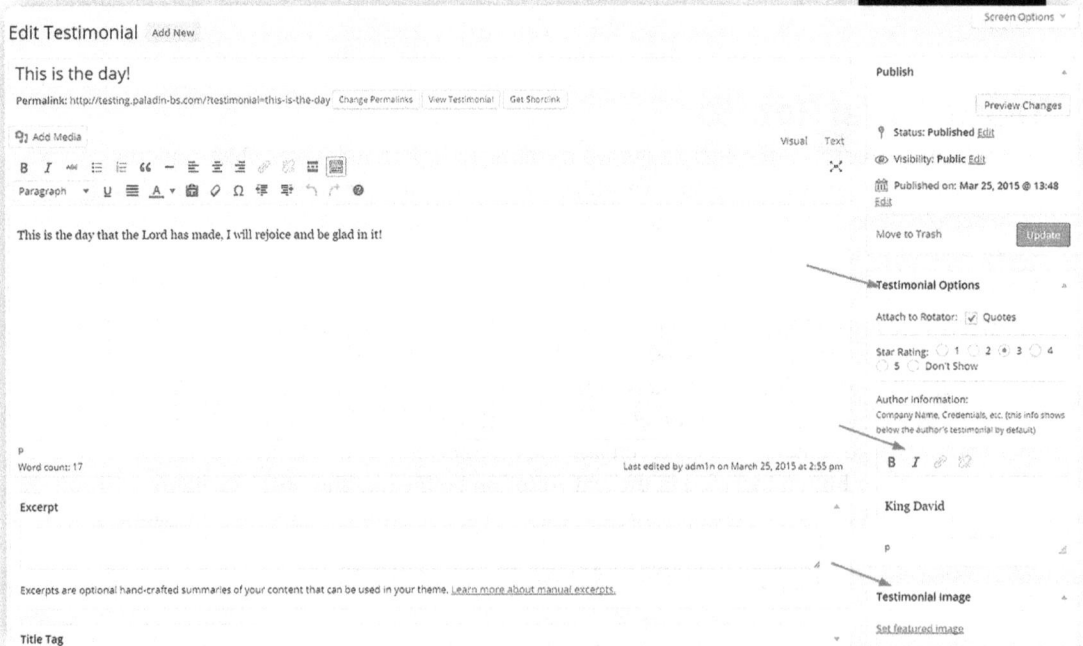

FIGURE 4.12

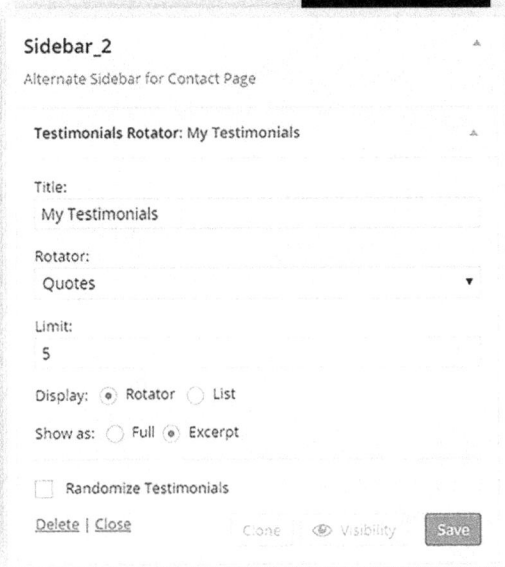

FIGURE 4.13

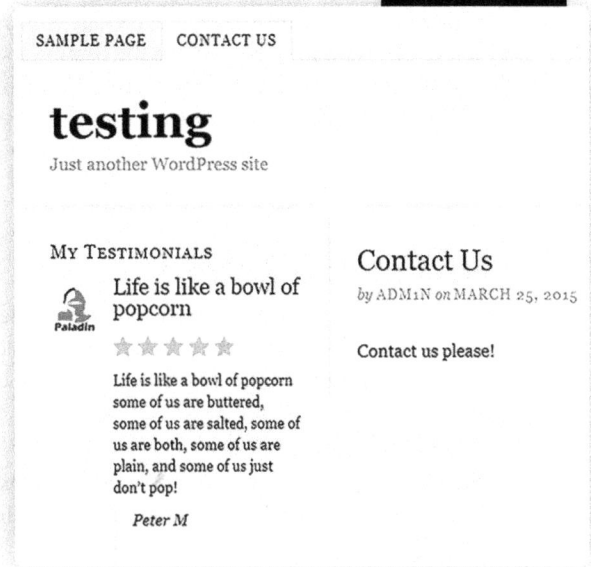

The widget area where these rotators can be deployed looks similar to the one in Figure 4.12. Here we can further configure how the rotator will appear in our sidebar. Figure 4.13 shows the widget in its deployed environment which is what our site visitors will see.

Simple Social Icons

What would the World Wide Web be without its social aspect? Pretty dull I would suspect. Enter *Simple Social Icons*[4]. This little plugin allows you to insert social icons and their destination URLs into a sidebar. It also allows you to control their color schemes and hover actions. See Figure 4.14.

FIGURE 4.14

[4]   *Simple Social Icons:*
   https://wordpress.org/plugins/simple-social-icons/

This plugin acts the same as the previous two we have discussed in that you simply drag and drop its widget control into the sidebar location you want and then add in the destination URLs for your social connections. As shown in figure 4.15, we have added example locations for all the provided social links in this plugin. Granted, you likely will not use all of them at the same time, but it's comforting to know you have all those options at your disposal as your web presence grows.

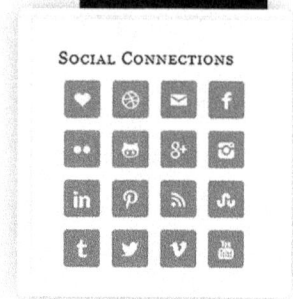

FIGURE 4.15

Two Column Admin

Two Column Admin is one of the plugins alluded to in the opening section of this chapter in that it does not have a specific menu entry created when installed. This is just a nice small plugin which allows for the admin dashboard to operate with two columns. By default, the dashboard only provides one column and if you have many reporting sections—like Google Analytics and Backup Buddy, etc—showing in the dashboard it makes for a lot of scrolling.

Shown in Figure 4.16 we see the screen options tab is exposed and the two column option is selected. Then the dashboard will display its contents in two columns.

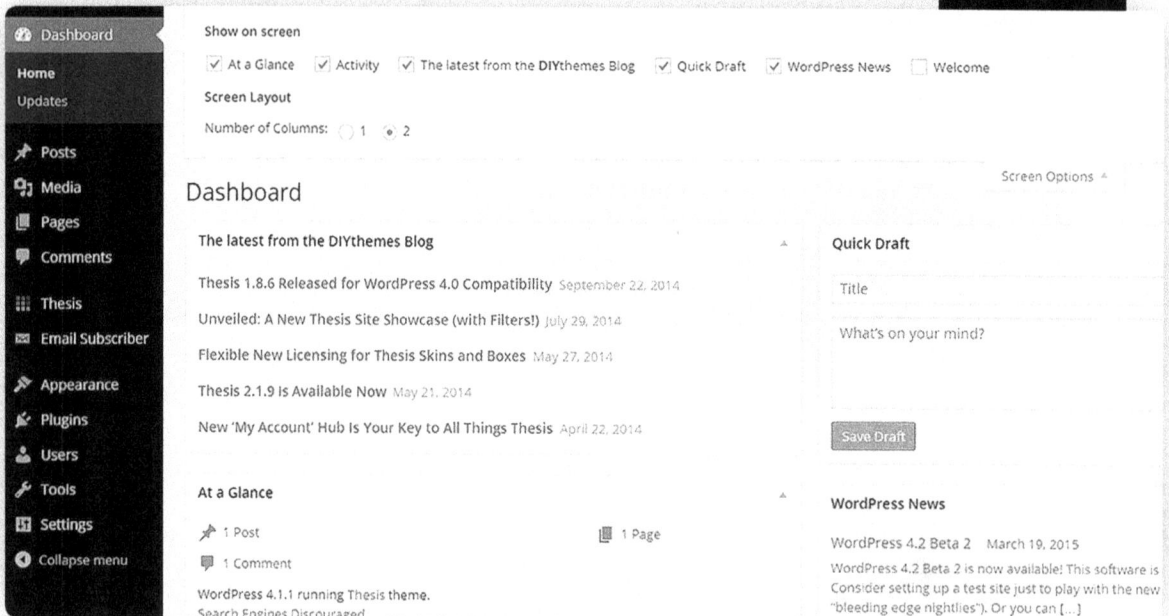

FIGURE 4.16

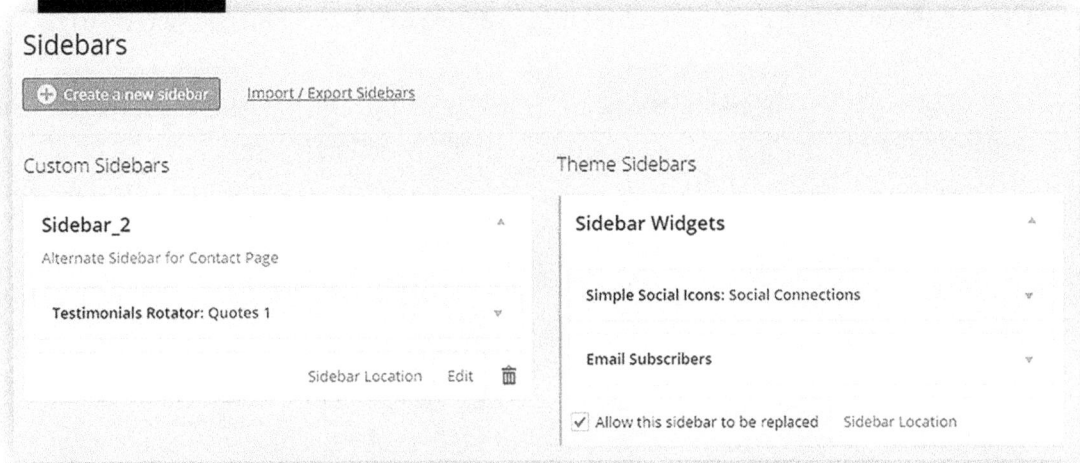

FIGURE 4.17

Custom Sidebars

The *Custom Sidebars*[5] plugin is a little more niche but very useful if employed well. It allows for different sidebars to be designed and implemented for different locations within your website. For example, you may have a portion of your site dedicated to ecommerce and you want some shopping cart widgets to only show up on those pages.

In our example here, we have simply created two different pages and assigned each page their own custom sidebar. This plugin takes over the widget area (again no admin menu additions) and allows you to name and create sidebars. Figure 4.17 shows these sidebars and the widgets for each one. *Sidebar_2* is the new one.

In Figure 4.18 you can see where it is assigned to the *Contact Us* page.

FIGURE 4.18

[5]   Custom Sidebars: https://wordpress.org/plugins/custom-sidebars/

Then, in Figures 4.19 and 4.20 you can see the two different sidebars for the two different pages.

FIGURE 4.19

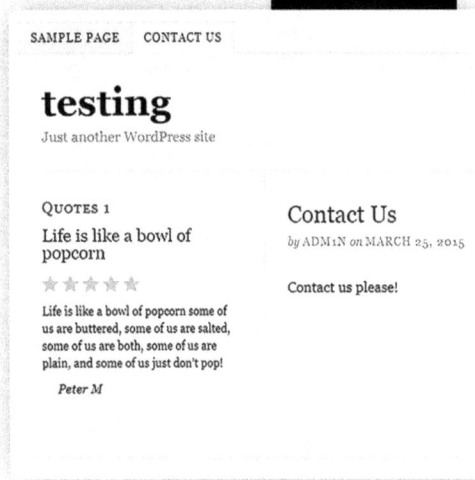

FIGURE 4.20

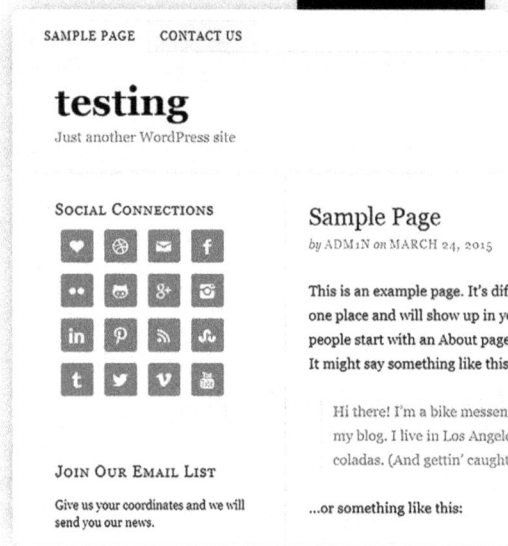

TinyMCE Color picker

TinyMCE Color picker[6] allows for more customization of the text you place within the editors of WordPress. Primarily this is the pages and posts areas but this is available anywhere you see an editor—composing email in email subscribers for example.

As you can see in Figure 4.21, where we are editing the *Contact Us* page, we can adjust both the foreground and background colors of text. The control for the foreground color is further enhanced by this plugin and it allows for better color selection; if you click the **add a color** option on the drop-down dialogue, you can even enter in hexadecimal color codes for exact color selections. This plugin also adds another drop-down button to the toolbar immediately to the right for setting background colors on your text. Again you can enter

FIGURE 4.21

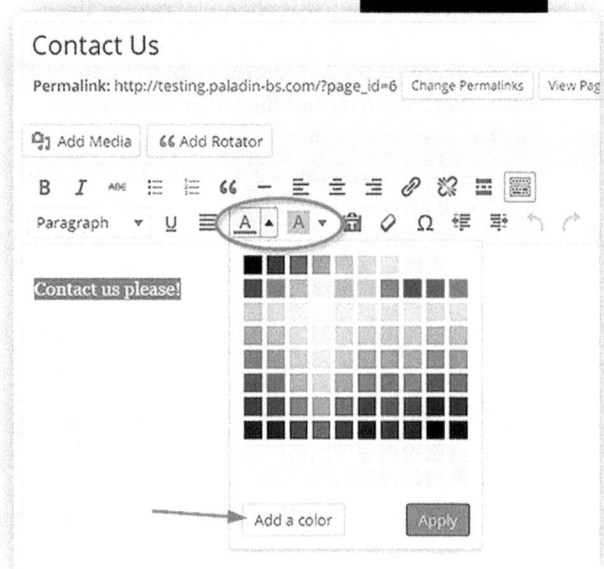

[6] *TinyMCE Color picker:* https://wordpress.org/plugins/tinymce-colorpicker/

hexadecimal values here if needed. The results of our little color adjustments are evident in Figure 4.22.

> Hexadecimal colors[7] are one way to specify combinations of how much red, green, and blue to mix to create a color. Typically they look like #ff000 for bright red or #ffffff for white.

Store Locator Plus

Store Locator Plus[8] is great for helping your site visitors find you physically on a map. It is usually placed on a contact, about, or similar page; however, it can be used for multiple locations. This plugin integrates with Google Maps. For example, if you're building a site for a local community college you could place a map locator for each location on campus where classes are being taught. If your site is for a church, you could make locations for the many places your satellite Bible studies are located. The options and permutations are endless really. Don't let the name fool you, if you aren't selling something you can still use this plugin.

After installing and activating you will see a top-level admin menu item named *Store Locator Plus*. Here the "Plus" refers to the commercial version of this plugin. All of the features included in this free version should be more than enough to get you started. Begin by clicking on the locations option and select **Add**. You will be presented with a screen like that shown in Figure 4.23.

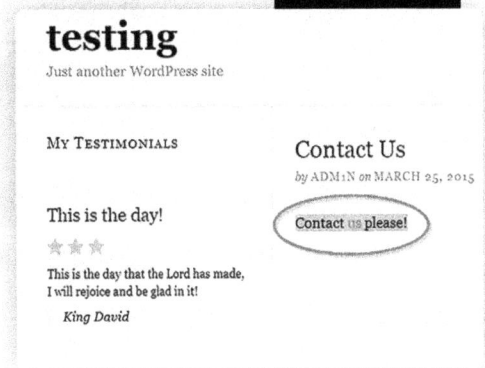

FIGURE 4.22

FIGURE 4.23

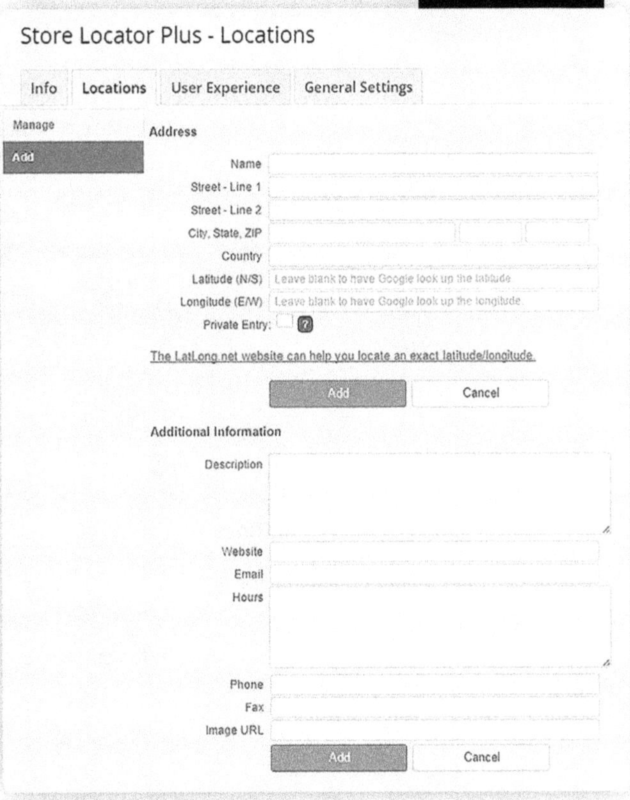

[7]   CSS Colors: http://www.w3schools.com/cssref/css_colors.asp
[8]   Store Locator Plus: https://wordpress.org/plugins/store-locator-le/

Enter all the pertinent information and save it. Next you want to control how this information shows on the map and how the map itself is displayed. To do this click on the *User Experience* menu option and then the *Map* sub-menu tab, as shown in Figure 4.24.

FIGURE 4.24

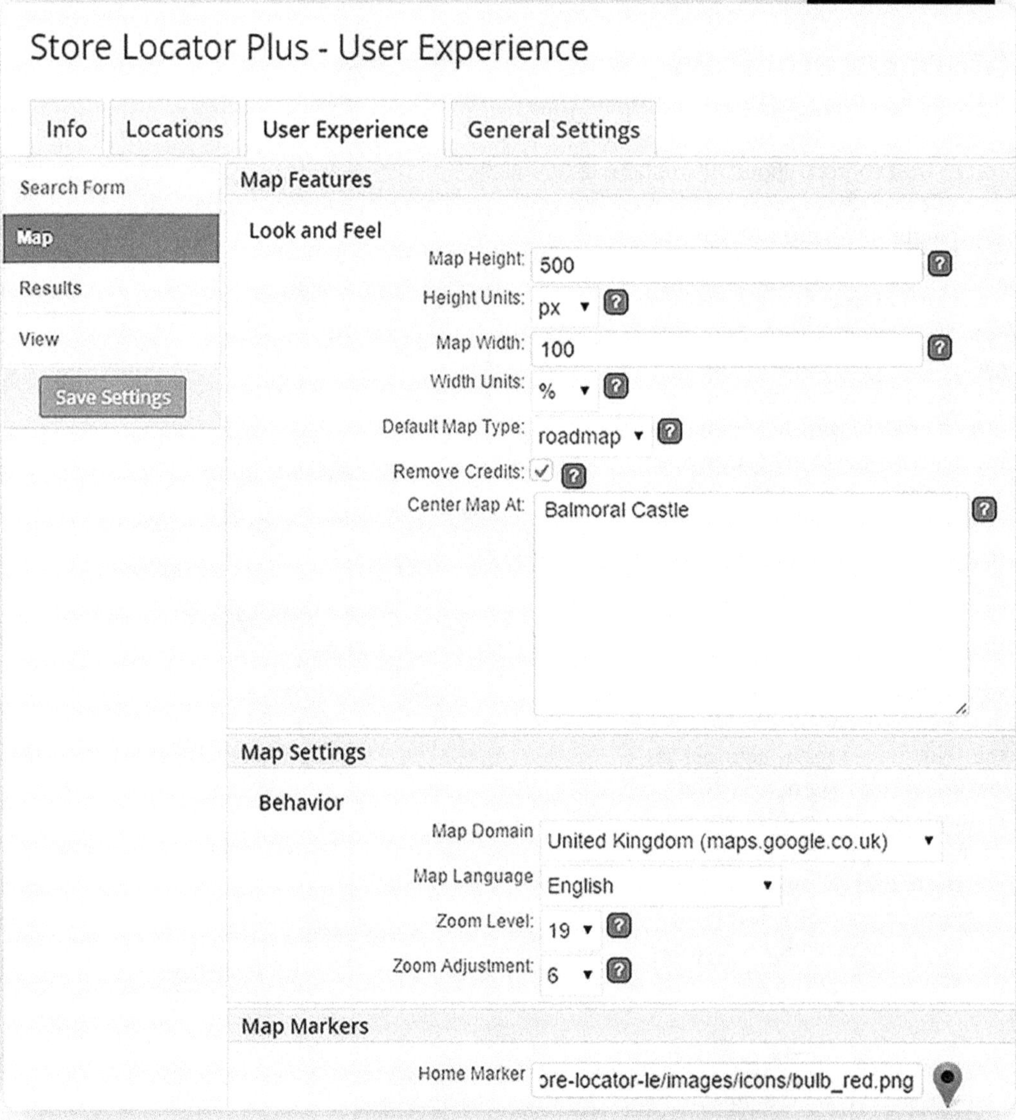

Here you can set the maps dimensions, the map type (satellite, street maps, etc.), the markers you want to use, as well as the map default location, language, and zoom levels. There are quite a few options here so be sure to try them all until you get what you want. Figure 4.25 shows the map location as added to the *Contact Us* page with Balmoral Castle in Scotland (the Queen of England's summer residence) as the starting point.

To use this locator on a page all you have to do is add the short code: [SL plus] to the text area and voila!

FIGURE 4.25

WP Currency Converter

WP Currency Converter[9] is a great plugin for having a tool to show currency exchange rates on your site. Especially if you are running a global ecommerce site you can pick a base currency and have worldwide visitors see what their selected items cost in their own currency. As mentioned in connection with the custom sidebar plugin earlier, you could limit the display of this plugin to a specific sidebar which only connects to the commerce portions of your site.

Figure 4.26 shows the widget's setup options and Figure 4.27 shows the plugin in action. This plugin gets its currency values from Google Finance on a regular basis.

FIGURE 4.26

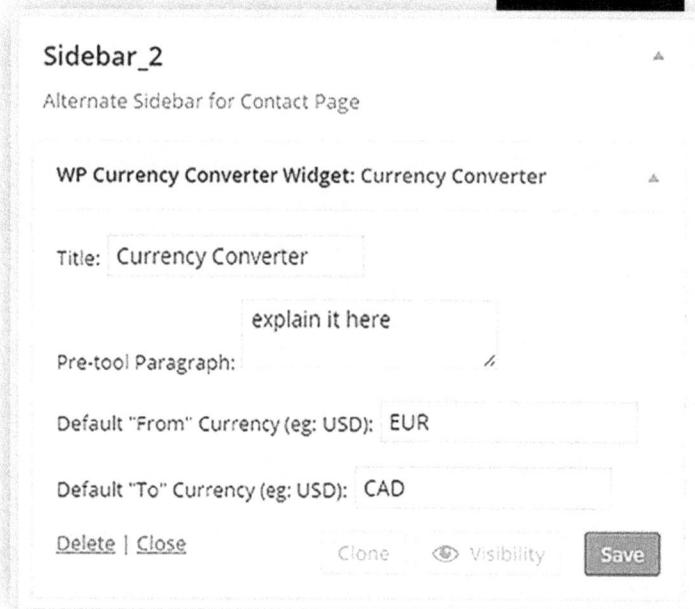

Sidebar_2
Alternate Sidebar for Contact Page

WP Currency Converter Widget: Currency Converter

Title: Currency Converter

Pre-tool Paragraph: explain it here

Default "From" Currency (eg: USD): EUR

Default "To" Currency (eg: USD): CAD

Delete | Close   Clone   Visibility   Save

FIGURE 4.27

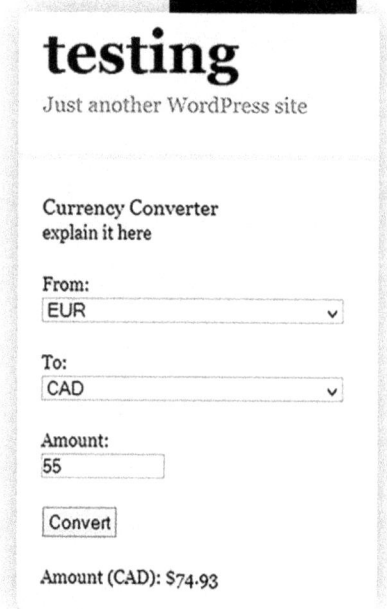

testing
Just another WordPress site

Currency Converter
explain it here

From:
EUR

To:
CAD

Amount:
55

Convert

Amount (CAD): $74.93

OpenHook

OpenHook[10] shows its value more in concert with the hooks sections of a WordPress theme. Basically, it allows you to enter your own custom PHP code almost anywhere. The one place we use it the most is in page footers where we supply PHP code to calculate the year portion of the current date as stored on the server. This allows us to have a constantly accurate copyright year displaying in our website's footer.

Note the example we are using here demands a WordPress user level which has permission to edit theme content, typically this would be Administrator level access.

[9]   WP Currency Converter: https://wordpress.org/plugins/wp-currency-converter/
[10]   OpenHook: https://wordpress.org/plugins/thesis-openhook/

After installing the plugin, in our Thesis skin editor (refer to the *Thesis specific chapter earlier*), we have to activate the "Open Box"—yes the name has changed—portion of this plugin, so go to **Thesis > Manage Boxes**, select the checkbox beside it and then click **Save Boxes**. This tells Thesis the plugin can be used within its template designer.

Now let's see how to make use of this plugin. Go to the home page footer template strip, accessed by **Thesis > Skin Editor** and then select **Page > Front Page** from the template button at the top left; this should look like Figure 4.28. We have some of the intermediate design strips collapsed for ease of viewing.

Hold down the shift key and drag off the two items currently there, namely *Attribution* and *WP Admin Link*, dropping them in the designated grey area on the top right. Pull down the list called *select a box to add* and choose **Open Box**. Click the blue **Add Box** button, then click the gears icon beside the open box name. Change the name to copyright_footer or whatever makes sense to you and click OK. You can ignore the *Programmatic ID* entry area for this example.

Shift and drag the box over to the template design service and drop it in the footer section. You should see something similar shown in Figure 4.29.

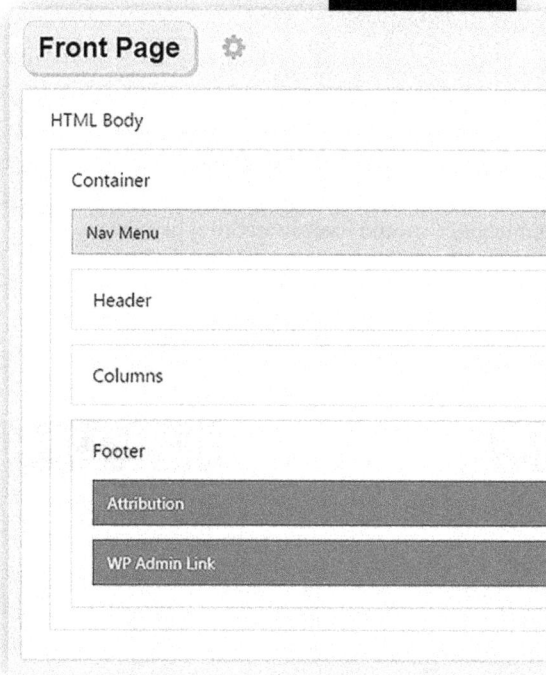

FIGURE 4.28

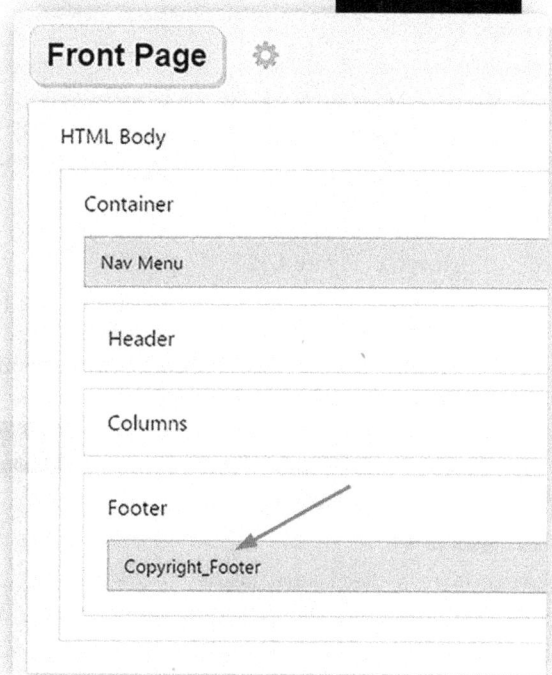

FIGURE 4.29

Click on **Save Template** and then when you get confirmation of the save being successful, click on **Thesis** (top right) to return to the standard admin environment. Next, click on **Thesis > Skin Content** and you should see the open box link on the provided list; Figure 4.30 shows this. Click on this link to open the code entry box.

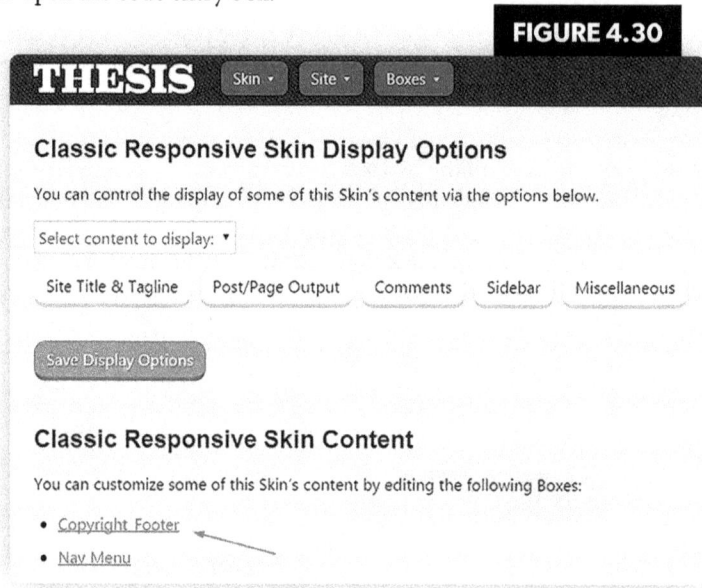

FIGURE 4.30

Here you can enter any raw text you want: CSS, HTML, straight text, and PHP code. In our example we just want to add the date year value and a little copyright message. You can see this in Figure 4.31.

Save your options when you are done and your public page should look something like that shown in Figure 4.32.

Now this may seem like a lot of work just for placing a custom copyright notice on your website, but remember you can add any type of code or text you want. Here we added some HTML, raw text, and PHP code. The customization freedom this open hook plugin provides is extremely valuable.

FIGURE 4.31

Copyright_Footer Options

Your Custom Code ⊘

```
<div style="float: left; text-align: left">
Copyright © <?php echo date("Y") ; ?> Testing Website - All Rights Reserved
<br />All trademarks are © by their respective owners
</div>
```

FIGURE 4.32

Copyright © 2015 Testing Website - All Rights Reserved
All trademarks are © by their respective owners

Please be sure to use this plugin with caution. *Remember it allows for the entry of raw PHP code into your site—"With great power comes great responsibility". If you're PHP code has a parse error, your site may crash with an error. A malicious plugin could find a way to insert its own PHP code using this capability. If you are doing a lot of custom work it is better to use themes, templates, and hooks as a more secure way to accomplish your tasks.*

WP Clone

WP Clone[11] has two major components to it. First, it allows for custom manual site backups and second, it can take these backups and restore them anywhere. This implies, as the plugin is aptly named, you can easily export your site from a development or staging site to a production site, but more on that later. The first capability of this plugin is to perform basic manual backups. Let's look at how this is accomplished. After install and activation you will see a new menu item added entitled *WP Clone*, click on this to view the plugin's interface, shown in Figure 4.33.

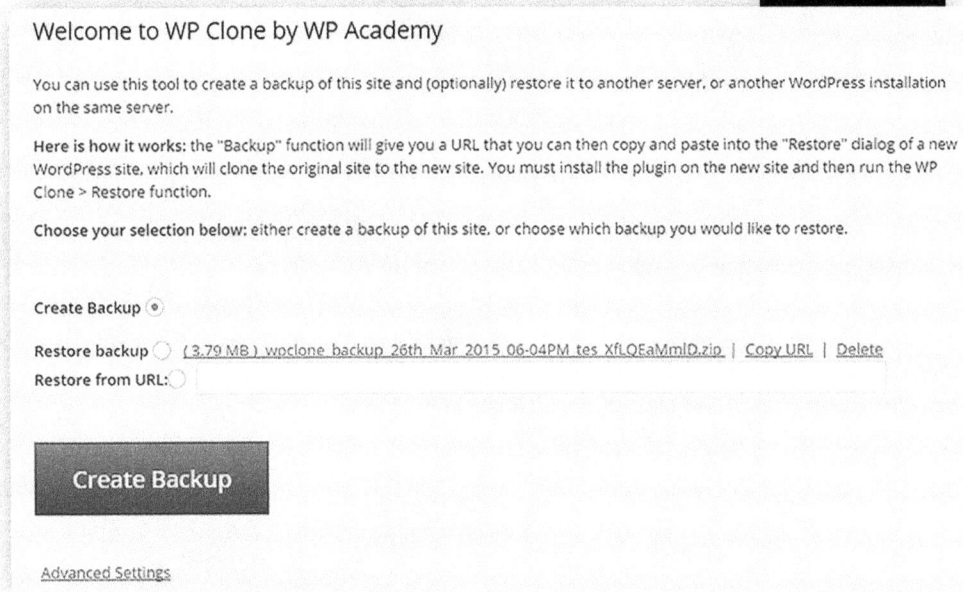

FIGURE 4.33

Welcome to WP Clone by WP Academy

You can use this tool to create a backup of this site and (optionally) restore it to another server, or another WordPress installation on the same server.

Here is how it works: the "Backup" function will give you a URL that you can then copy and paste into the "Restore" dialog of a new WordPress site, which will clone the original site to the new site. You must install the plugin on the new site and then run the WP Clone > Restore function.

Choose your selection below: either create a backup of this site, or choose which backup you would like to restore.

Create Backup ⦿

Restore backup ◯ (3.79 MB) wpclone_backup_26th_Mar_2015_06-04PM_tes_XfLQEaMmID.zip | Copy URL | Delete
Restore from URL: ◯

Create Backup

Advanced Settings

Without getting into the advanced options, simply click on the big blue **Create Backup** button and after a warning it may take some time to assemble, not only is your site backed up but also your underlying connected database. You can control this more accurately in the advanced setting area. You'll be informed your backup is successful when the process completes. Then the backup file is added to the list of any other existing backups and you can either restore from that backup, download the file by clicking on it, copy the URL to use elsewhere, or delete it.

[11] *WP Clone: https://wordpress.org/plugins/wp-clone-by-wp-academy/*

The other really valuable feature of this plugin is the clone function. Once you have completed a backup, one of your options is to *Copy URL*. This allows you to take the URL and its connected backup data and move it wholesale (clone it) to another site. The only caveat here is you also need to have WP clone installed on the target site. That means a basic setup of WordPress also has to be up and running on the target location. Going to said target, one then merely pastes the URL into the *Restore* single line entry, clicks the agreement box (after you read it!), and presses **Restore from URL**. The cloning process begins. See Figure 4.34 for an example.

FIGURE 4.34

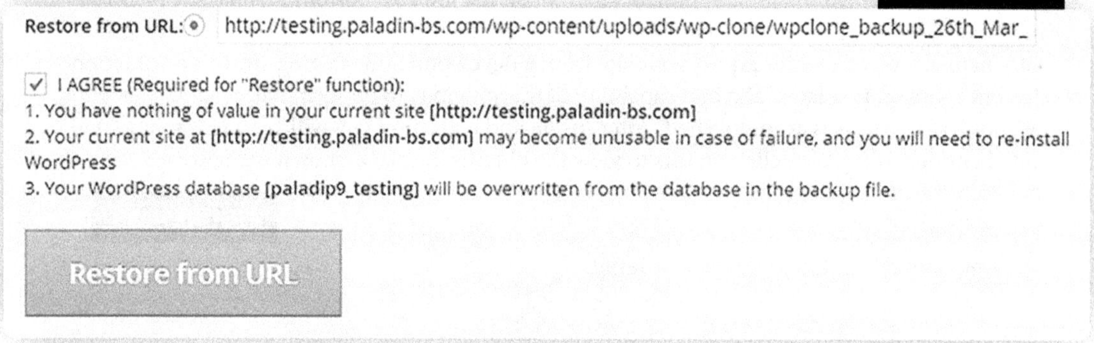

Restore from URL: ● http://testing.paladin-bs.com/wp-content/uploads/wp-clone/wpclone_backup_26th_Mar_

✓ I AGREE (Required for "Restore" function):
1. You have nothing of value in your current site [http://testing.paladin-bs.com]
2. Your current site at [http://testing.paladin-bs.com] may become unusable in case of failure, and you will need to re-install WordPress
3. Your WordPress database [paladip9_testing] will be overwritten from the database in the backup file.

Restore from URL

One thing to remember is you are taking a complete copy of the source site to the target site and therefore any usernames, passwords, posts, pages, and anything else will totally replace your target site. So be sure there is nothing of value on your target site and be sure there is nothing in the source site you don't want displayed or active on the new target site.

Note: WP Clone takes some time to run its routines depending on the overall content of your site, so be sure to verify your host allows for longer running scripts (a longer timeout setting). This plugin may fail altogether on sites with larger content; check the plugin's FAQ[12] for current limitations and preferred hosts.

[12]   *WP Clone FAQ: http://members.wpacademy.com/wpclone-faq/*

FileBrowser

The *FileBrowser*[13] plugin (note spelling with no space) allows for a file level interface from within WordPress administration. Similar to a traditional file manager interface, you can add new files (upload), browse to and create new folders, download files (by clicking on a filename), delete, copy, and move files. You can even edit the files directly within the admin interface. See Figure 4.35 for a sample of this interface.

FIGURE 4.35

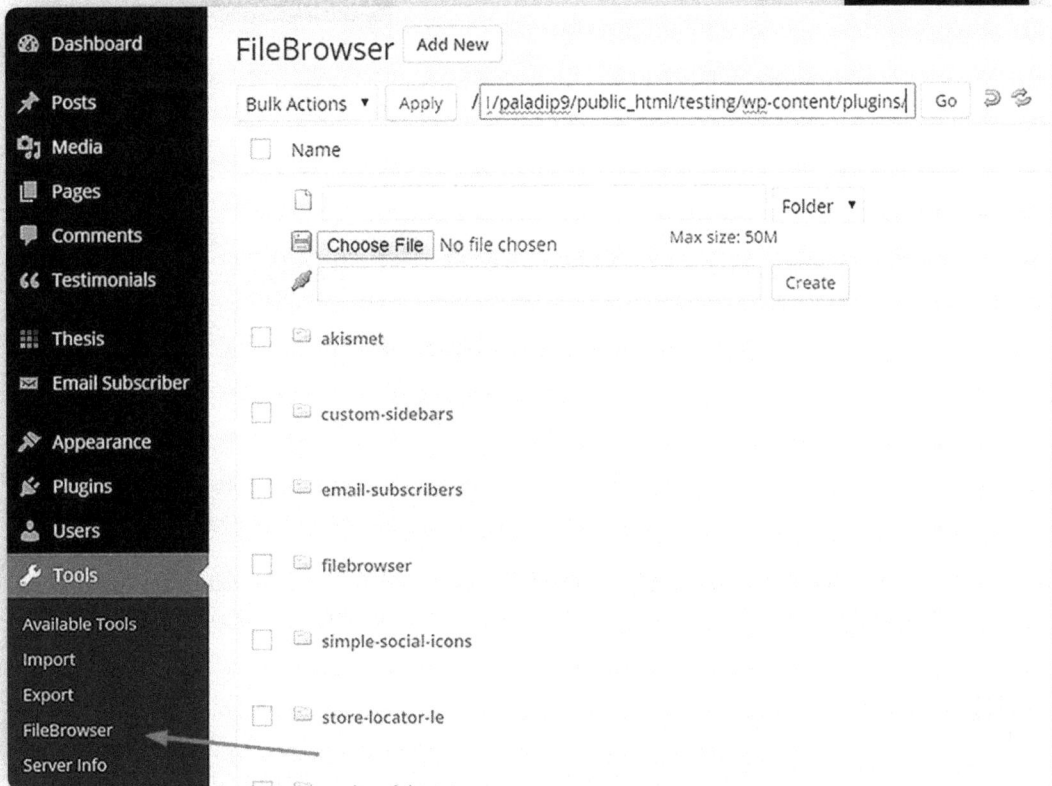

Of course, with such great power comes great responsibility so be very careful using this plugin as you could unintentionally cripple your website with just a few errant clicks. The file browser can be accessed under the tools menu.

[13]   FileBrowser: https://wordpress.org/plugins/filebrowser/

Simple Maintenance

Many times in the life of a website you will want to temporarily disable the public interface while doing simple updates or layout changes in your admin area. You don't want your site visitors to see any partially complete pages so you should make good use of the *Simple Maintenance*[14] plugin. After installation and activation your site is automatically placed in maintenance mode. Figure 4.36 shows what the homepage of your public site would then look like.

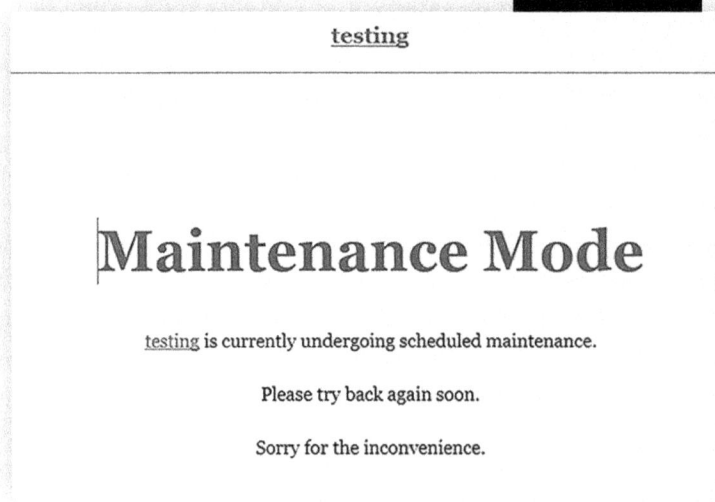

FIGURE 4.36

testing

Maintenance Mode

testing is currently undergoing scheduled maintenance.

Please try back again soon.

Sorry for the inconvenience.

If you want to adjust this look, simply select edit from the link under the plugin name on the *Installed plugins* page and select the `sm-template.php` file. To reactivate your site to full operation merely deactivate this plugin.

Add From Server

Another great plugin to consider is *Add From Server*[15]. Many times, web hosts place a limit on the file size of media, and files in general, that are uploaded via web forms. This plugin gets around such limitations. After installing and activating the plugin you should see *Add From Server* on the Settings menu. Clicking on that menu item will bring up the options page for you to adjust as needed—see Figure 4.37 for a sample.

You can restrict the user level that can perform large file uploads as well as where these files can be placed, so be sure to carefully consider the where and who of this plugin.

[14]   *Simple Maintenance:* https://wordpress.org/plugins/simple-maintenance/
[15]   *Add From Server:* https://wordpress.org/plugins/add-from-server/

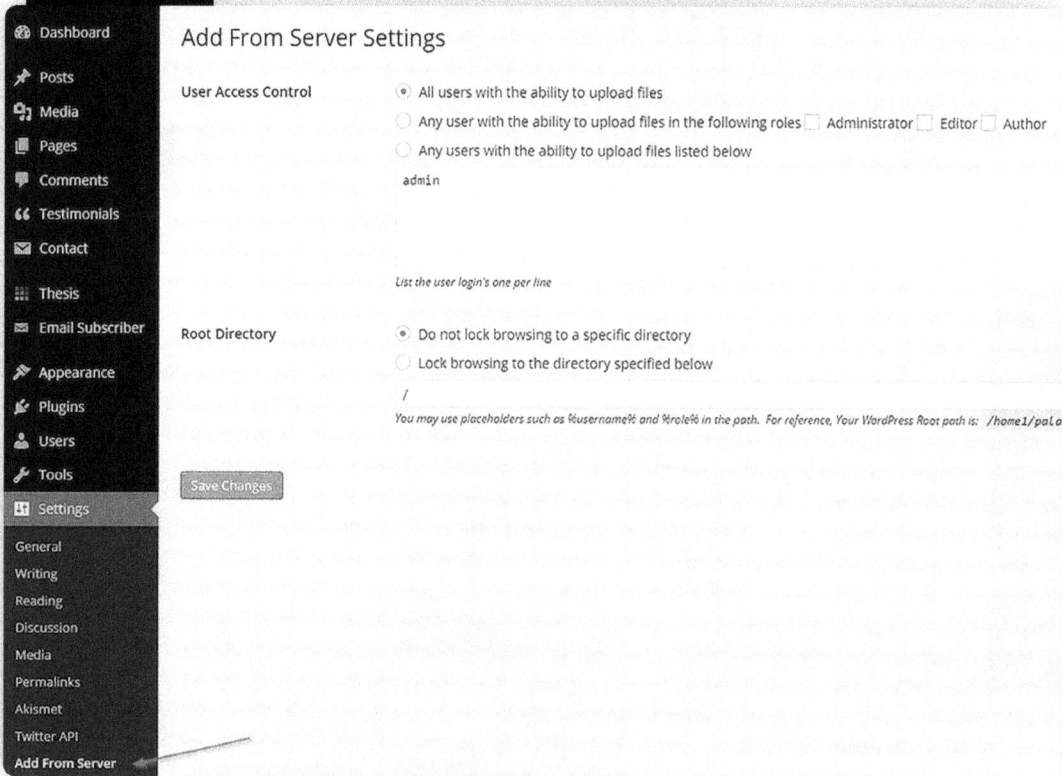

FIGURE 4.37

Add From Server Settings

User Access Control
- ⦿ All users with the ability to upload files
- ◯ Any user with the ability to upload files in the following roles ☐ Administrator ☐ Editor ☐ Author
- ◯ Any users with the ability to upload files listed below

admin

List the user login's one per line

Root Directory
- ⦿ Do not lock browsing to a specific directory
- ◯ Lock browsing to the directory specified below

/

You may use placeholders such as %username% and %role% in the path. For reference, Your WordPress Root path is: /home1/palo

Save Changes

Once you have your plugin configured as you want, you can start uploading larger files (this has to be done via an S/FTP client) and subsequently place them in your site's media library. A new menu item is also placed under the media item also called *Add From Server*. Here you can navigate to the folder you have uploaded the large file to and import it into WordPress' Media library.

WordPress Popup

The next great plugin to take a look at is *WordPress Popup*[16]. This does exactly what you would expect based on its name. This plugin allows for popup messages to be displayed on your site. Some designers and website visitors consider this kind of "interruption" to be annoying, so use sparingly. However, it is included here because there are definitely use-cases for it. Consider you want to conduct a survey, prompt visitors to join your mailing list, or you have a special discount on a product in your online store. There is a place for this plugin, but don't be a pest with it.

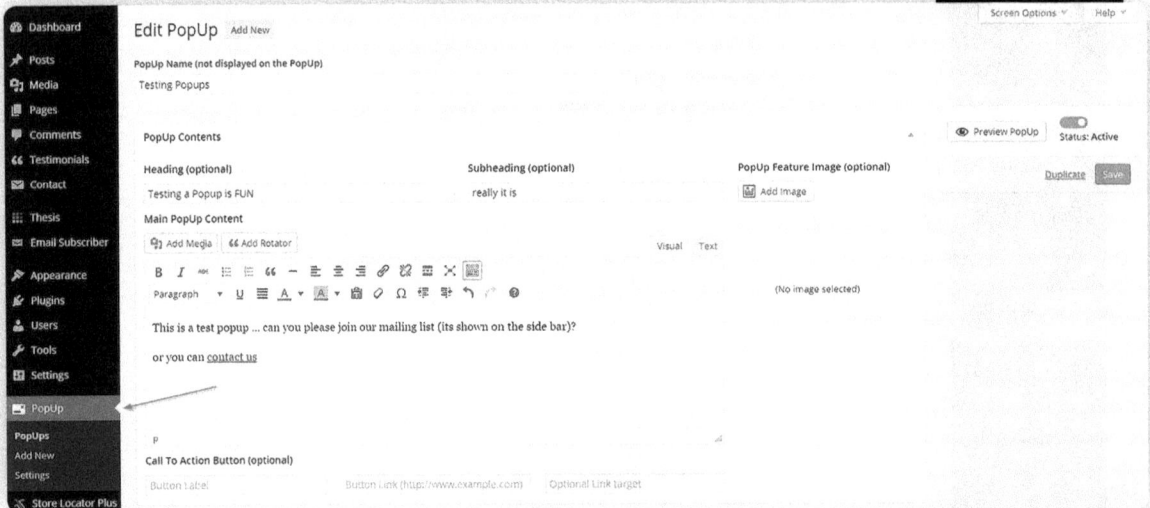

FIGURE 4.38

Install and activate the plugin and you will see a new menu item added to the admin area called *PopUp*. Here you can add multiple popups and control when and how they appear. Figure 4.38 and 4.39 show one in the process of being configured and then being displayed on the public site. There are a lot of settings and controls you can set on these popups: adding a "never show again" control, changing the CSS of the popup, adding an image, specifying how the popup

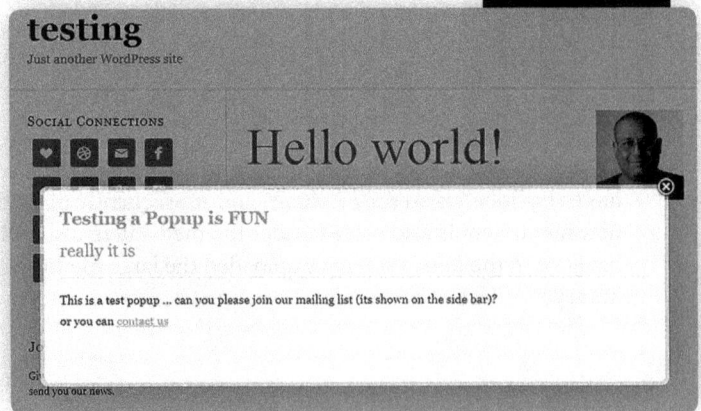

FIGURE 4.39

[16]   *WordPress Popup:* https://wordpress.org/plugins/wordpress-popup/

shows up and how it closes down (animations), if they should appear on mobile devices, and so on. So be sure to test these options out and make sure your popups are efficient and effective.

Simple Links

Simple Links[17] is another plugin to consider. It offers a nice, clean way to manage and display your site's links to other web sites or web resources. Install and activate the plugin and you will see a new menu item called (oddly enough) *Simple Links*. You can set broad settings in the *Settings* sub-menu and arrange the order in which they appear in the *Link Ordering* area. You can also manage your links by categories if you so desire (Link Categories sub-menu). Most importantly you can add links with **Add New Links**. The creation of a new link is shown in Figure 4.40.

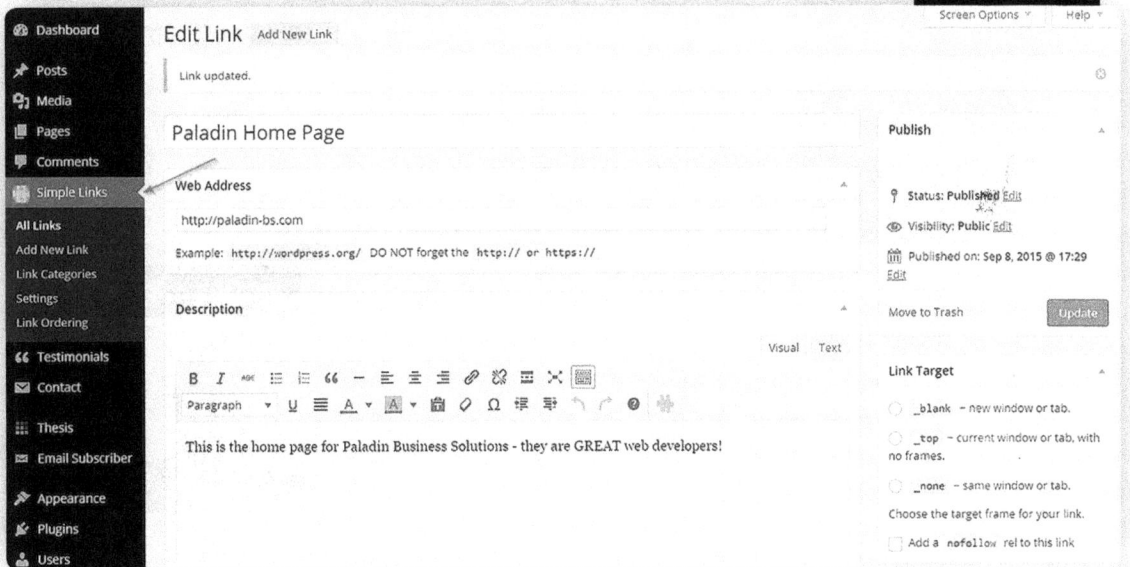

FIGURE 4.40

These links are then listed on a page you create. Here we called it *Simple Links* and we simply added in a short code like this:

```
[simple-links description="true"]
```

[17] Simple Links: https://wordpress.org/plugins/simple-links/

See Figure 4.41. The controlling of the display is managed by the different options added to the short code. Navigate to the plugin's support page *https://matlipe.com/simple-links-docs/* for details on the many short code options available.

Figure 4.42 shows the display of the links list on the public site.

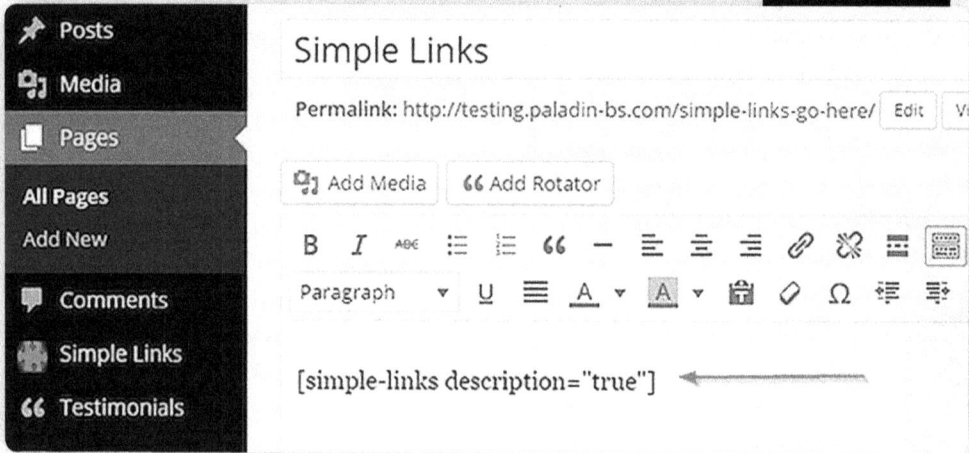

FIGURE 4.41

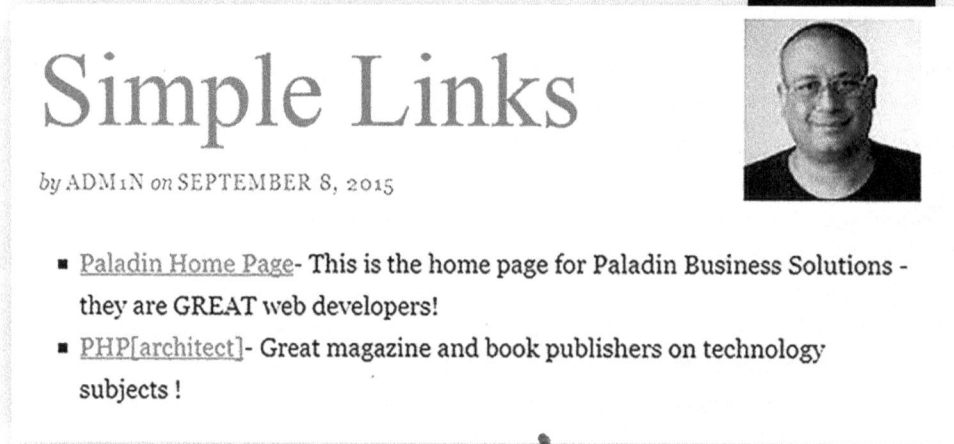

FIGURE 4.42

Easy Twitter Feed Widget (Other Social Feeds)

The last plugin we'll look at in this chapter will be an example on the theme of social media feeds. Here we will be looking to integrate Twitter content feed, but this will be very similar in concept to the other social feeds like Instagram, Pinterest, LinkedIn, Flickr, and Facebook (there are many more for sure). Here we want to have our site pick up the Twitter data that we are feeding to an unsuspecting and unappreciative world. When we add notes and comments to Twitter our site will pick up that content and add it in set time intervals (cache time). Figure 4.43 shows the Easy Twitter Feed Widget plugin being added into the sidebar widget area.

You have to provide your twitter handle and a Twitter widget ID in order for your feed to be authenticated and picked up. This is accessed in WordPress admin by doing the following:

1. Sign In to your Twitter Account
2. Go to Settings > Widgets > Create new
3. Click the Create Widget button
4. You can copy the Widget ID from Browser Address Bar e.g. 4191XXXXXX99552
5. OR You can copy the Widget ID from the given HTML under the Widget Preview i.e. `data-widget-id="4191XXXXXX99552"`

Once you are authenticated you can save your widget settings and then take a look at the live site. Figure 4.44 shows a feed being displayed on the widget side bar.

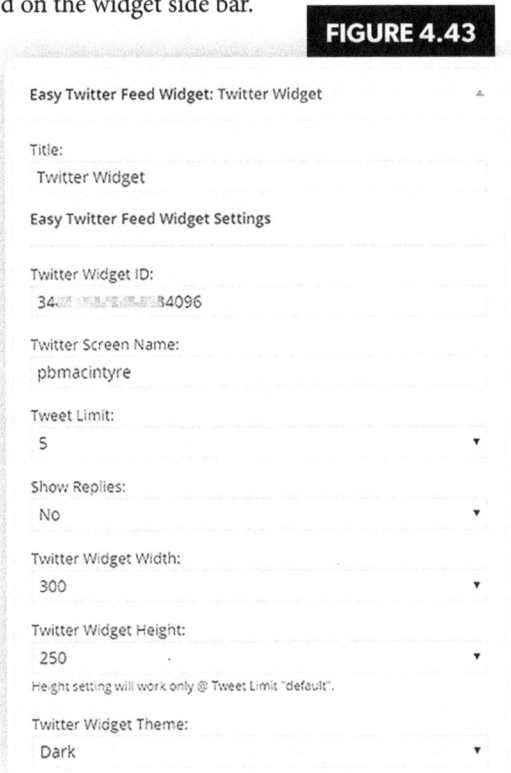

FIGURE 4.44

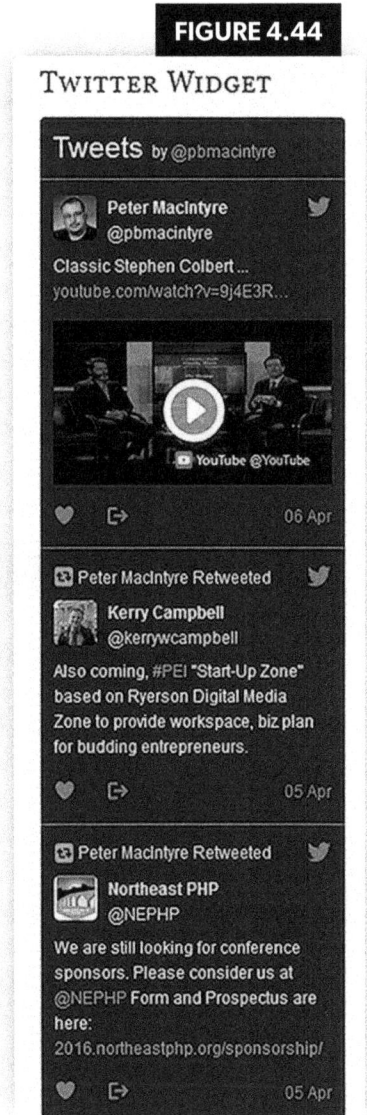

FIGURE 4.43

Chapter 5

The Best Plugins—Part 2 Advanced Tasks

This chapter focuses on some of the best plugins existing for more complex tasks. The plugins for short simple tasks are covered in the previous chapter. Here we will talk about large scale plugins like ecommerce, search engine optimization (SEO), site protection, memberships, and Google Analytics just to name a few.

You have to consider whether these plugins should be installed on your site as they take a lot of space in most cases and they take a long time to set up and to fine tune. We won't be going into every detail for each plugin here, so if you do decide to use one or more of these "larger" plugins try to install them on a testing site so you will have a playpen area as you learn. It's best not to experiment on a live environment.

Wordfence Security

The short description of *Wordfence Security*[1] from its creators is as follows:

"The Wordfence WordPress security plugin provides free enterprise-class WordPress security, protecting your website from hacks and malware."

This is a good plugin to have regardless of the subject matter of your site. Look for this plugin by the full name *Wordfence Security* and install it. Once you activate it you will be offered a tour and will be requested to provide an email address to the plugin itself so it can send you notifications from your own site on any issues it may discover. Take the tour if you like, but be sure to provide your email address as it will be used to send notices and warnings as Wordfence does its thing. Enter your email address and click **get started**, you may want to turn off the security email newsletter option beforehand, then click close if you are not taking the product tour. See Figure 5.1 for what this dialog looks like.

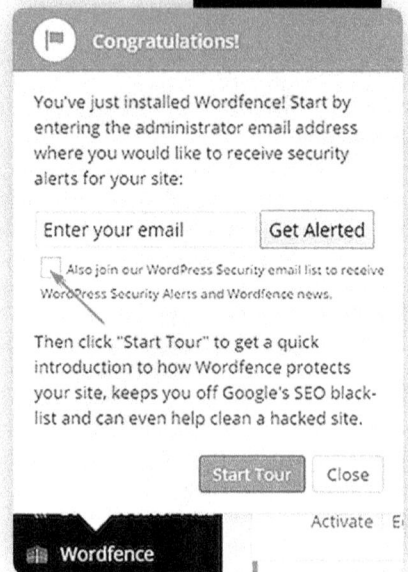

FIGURE 5.1

Next, comes the complex array of options. Select **Wordfence** > **Options** to open this page. The top of this page is shown in Figure 5.2. Let's highlight the key features of this powerful plugin.

Note: Once you have this plugin set up the way you want, be sure to use the export/import feature at the bottom of the options page to easily set up this plugin on other WordPress sites. You'll find this to be a big time saver.

Note: On most of the options here you will see a small information icon linking to further descriptions and help about what the specific item is meant to accomplish. If you are not sure what a feature does, simply click this icon and you will be taken to the Wordfence documentation site for more detail on the topic in question.

Under *Basic options* be sure you turn on the first two options namely *enable firewall* and *login security*. *Enable firewall* performs the following protections:

- Country Blocking (premium customers only) tries to block traffic from specific countries.
- Throttling limits how often some visitors can access features of your site
- IP blocking will block traffic from specific IP addresses
- Brute force attack protection

[1]   *Wordfence Security:* https://wordpress.org/plugins/wordfence/

- Two-factor authentication (cellphone sign-in–premium customers only) will have users confirm a short code or number typically sent via text before they can log in.
- All other firewall rules, including the rules under advanced blocking where ranges of IPs are blocked and user-agent patterns are blocked

The second one, *login security*, performs the following protections:

- Enforcement of strong passwords
- Locking users out after a defined number of login failures
- Locking out users after a number of forgotten password retrieval attempts
- Locking out invalid usernames
- Preventing WordPress from revealing valid usernames in login errors
- Preventing username discovery through author scans
- Immediate blocking of IPs who try to sign in as a defined list of usernames

You should seriously consider turning on *enable automatic schedule scans* and *update Wordfence automatically*. The first option scans your site once every 24 hours (you get to choose the time of day if you are a premium customer), and the second one simply updates the Wordfence plugin with updates as they are released–always a good idea to protect against newer vulnerabilities. Do your own research on the other basic options and "season to taste".

Under the alert section I typically turn on options 2 to 5 as these options are only triggered when there is a perceived issue with the site.

FIGURE 5.2

Wordfence Options
Learn more about Wordfence Options

Wordfence Live Activity: Idle

License

Your Wordfence API Key:	0cac0bd00c4b5e39b9d35fb93e989841963814a22b817c5f11318c9127090c8e44af41695a
Key type currently active:	The currently active API Key is a Free Key. Click Here to Upgrade to Wordfence Premium now.

Basic Options

Enable firewall	✓ NOTE: This checkbox enables ALL firewall functions including IP, country and advanced blocking and the "Firewall Rules" below.
Enable login security	✓ This option enables all "Login Security" options. You can modify individual options further down this page.
Enable Live Traffic View	✓ This option enables live traffic logging.
Advanced Comment Spam Filter	☐ Premium Feature In addition to free comment filtering (see below) this option filters comments against several additional real-time lists of known spammers and infected hosts.
Check if this website is being "Spamvertised"	☐ Premium Feature When doing a scan, Wordfence will check with spam services if your site domain name is appearing as a link in spam emails.
Check if this website IP is generating spam	☐ Premium Feature When doing a scan, Wordfence will check with spam services if your website IP address is listed as a known source of spam email.
Enable automatic scheduled scans	✓ Regular scans ensure your site stays secure.
Update Wordfence automatically when a new version is released?	✓ Automatically updates Wordfence to the newest version within 24 hours of a new release.

The following image shows a typical email Wordfence generates. Here it is calling for its own update. Depending on your notification settings, you could get a lot of email, so either set up a filter on your email system to automatically deal with email coming from Wordfence or create a new email address specifically for this purpose.

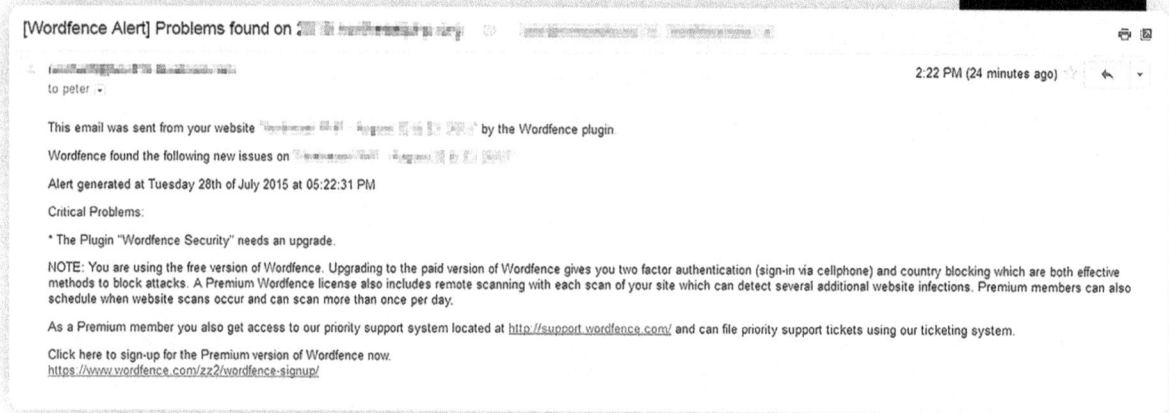

[Wordfence Alert] Problems found on

2:22 PM (24 minutes ago)

to peter

This email was sent from your website by the Wordfence plugin.

Wordfence found the following new issues on

Alert generated at Tuesday 28th of July 2015 at 05:22:31 PM

Critical Problems:

* The Plugin "Wordfence Security" needs an upgrade.

NOTE: You are using the free version of Wordfence. Upgrading to the paid version of Wordfence gives you two factor authentication (sign-in via cellphone) and country blocking which are both effective methods to block attacks. A Premium Wordfence license also includes remote scanning with each scan of your site which can detect several additional website infections. Premium members can also schedule when website scans occur and can scan more than once per day.

As a Premium member you also get access to our priority support system located at http://support.wordfence.com/ and can file priority support tickets using our ticketing system.

Click here to sign-up for the Premium version of Wordfence now.
https://www.wordfence.com/zz2/wordfence-signup/

Google Analytics Dashboard for WP

Google does a superb job of collecting site statistical information. The only drawback to their analytic data collection is you have to go to their site to see the collected information. The next plugin we are looking at is called *Google Analytics Dashboard for WP*[2]. This plugin makes a connection to your Google account, draws in most of the analytical data, and presents it to you within the Administration area of your WordPress site.

You may also be interested in a similar plugin called Google Analytics by Yoast as it does much the same tasks as the one in focus here. Google Analytics Dashboard for WP in our opinion has a better user interface and presents more meaningful data.

If you do indeed use the *Google Analytics Dashboard for WP* plugin, then there is no real need for adding the Google Analytics information into Thesis. On the Thesis top menu go to **Site > Google Analytics** and remove any codes that are here and then save your changes.

After you install and activate this plugin you will see *Google Analytics* added to the admin menu close to the bottom of the list. Figure 5.4 shows you this with its expanded sub-menu.

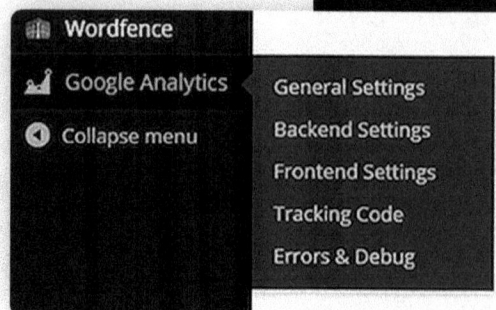

Wordfence

Google Analytics · General Settings

Collapse menu · Backend Settings

Frontend Settings

Tracking Code

Errors & Debug

[2]   Google Analytics Dashboard for WP: https://wordpress.org/plugins/google-analytics-dashboard-for-wp/

The first thing you have to is to make the connection between this plugin and your Google Analytics account. So all you have to do is to go to the General Settings menu and click on the **Authorize Plugin** button. A new screen will appear showing you a link to get your access code. Click on the link and you will be asked to login to your Google account and then you'll be presented with a code about 45 characters long. Figure 5.5 shows this process. Once you have your code saved the screen will refresh and you will see your website name being tracked and your Tracking ID, as well as some other identifying information which helps to prove you are tracking the right website.

FIGURE 5.5

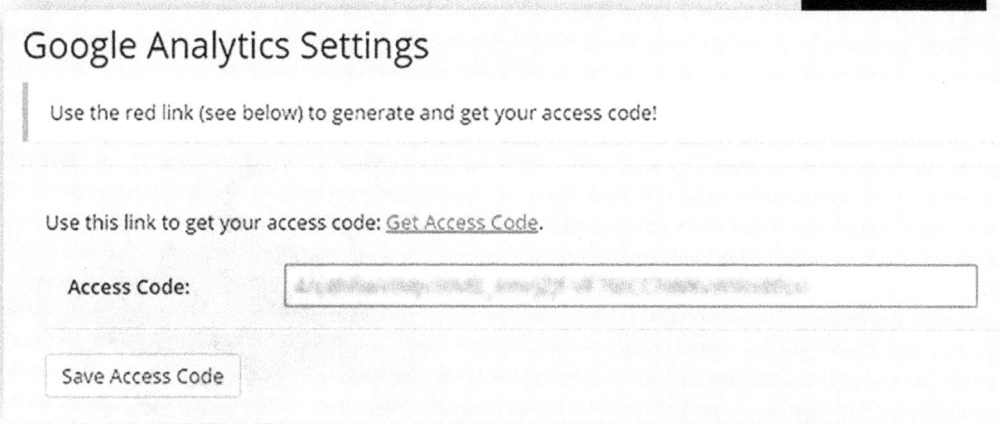

Check the Backend and Frontend settings pages to ensure you have those set to what you want. You can limit some of the tracking properties and who you allow to see the statistics.

The next area you want to look at is the dashboard area itself. This is where this plugin really shows its value. Click on the Dashboard menu at the top of the admin interface to reveal the admin dashboard.

Figures 5.6 and 5.7 show the different combinations of Analytics data which can be displayed.

FIGURE 5.6

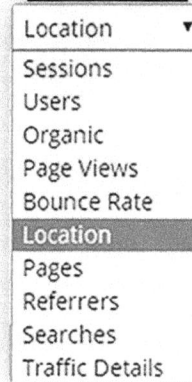

FIGURE 5.7

Figure 5.8 shows the display for the last 30 days by location on a world map with the numbers of visitors by named country showing below the map.

FIGURE 5.8

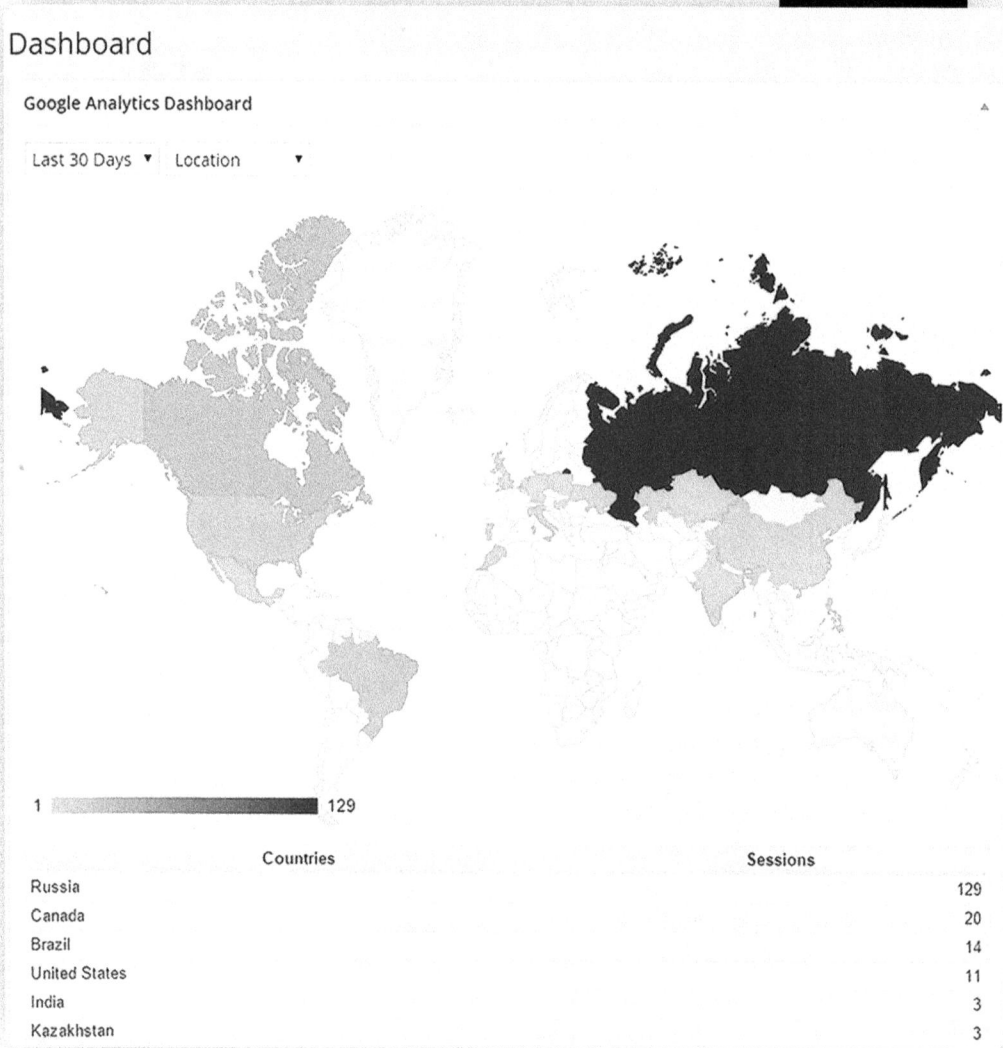

Dashboard

Google Analytics Dashboard

Last 30 Days ▾ | Location ▾

Countries	Sessions
Russia	129
Canada	20
Brazil	14
United States	11
India	3
Kazakhstan	3

This kind of data can be very helpful when you are looking at your overall site health and statistics. Who visited your site from where and when can help you with specifying and targeting your next marketing campaign for example.

Figure 5.9 shows the number of page views with their respective individual counts when the data style drop down is changed to *Pages*. The selections and combinations can go on for some time, so be sure to explore all the options this plugin offers and make good use of the traffic data it provides.

Note the data and pages shown here are from a live site.

FIGURE 5.9

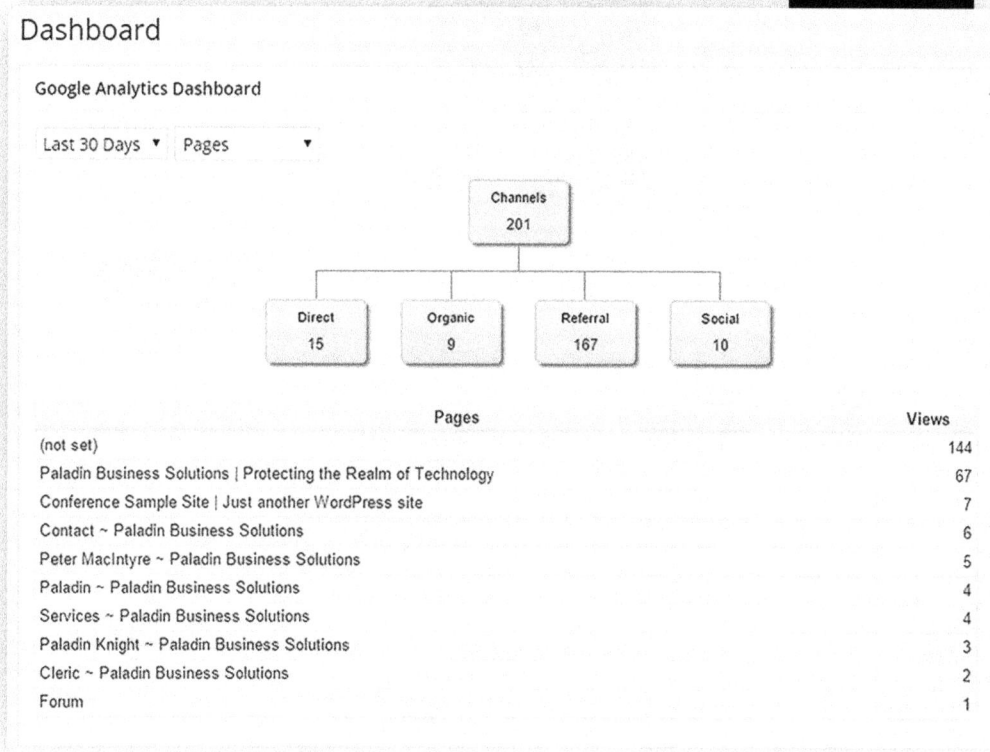

Pages	Views
(not set)	144
Paladin Business Solutions	Protecting the Realm of Technology	67
Conference Sample Site	Just another WordPress site	7
Contact ~ Paladin Business Solutions	6
Peter MacIntyre ~ Paladin Business Solutions	5
Paladin ~ Paladin Business Solutions	4
Services ~ Paladin Business Solutions	4
Paladin Knight ~ Paladin Business Solutions	3
Cleric ~ Paladin Business Solutions	2
Forum	1

Contact Form 7 / Contact Form DB

Contact Form 7[3] is the next major plugin to consider. This is a tool used to create forms on your site so visitors can contact you or leave other forms of communication. After you install and activate this plugin the menu item labeled *Contact* will be added to the admin menu. Clicking on the menu item opens the listing of all existing forms (one is given to you upon initial installation). You can create as many new forms as you like by clicking **Add New** at the top of the page. Figure 5.10 shows this listing page and Figure 5.11 shows an existing form in edit mode.

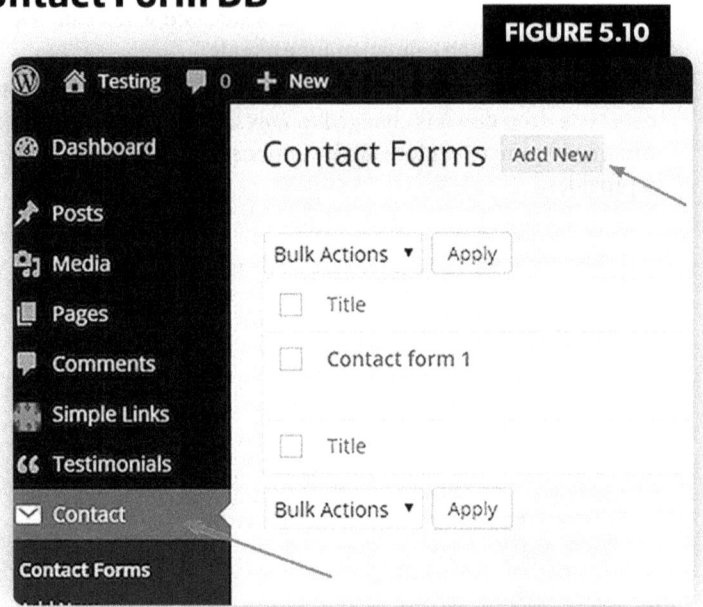

FIGURE 5.10

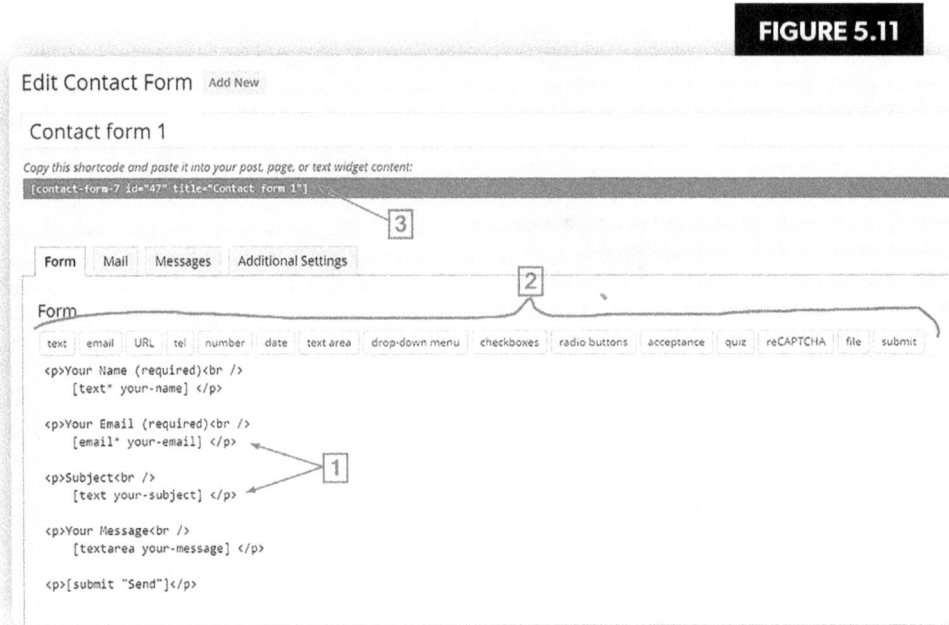

FIGURE 5.11

[3]   Contact Form 7: https://wordpress.org/plugins/contact-form-7/

The basic form you get when installing the plugin is called "contact form 1" it has a basic layout of a typical contact form prebuilt for you. As seen in Figure 5.11, the markup of the form [1] is a combination of HTML tags and form element short codes like [email* your-email]. Across the top of this forum editor area [2] you will see a series of buttons which can insert more form data collecting elements. Numbers, dates, checkboxes, radio buttons, reCAPTCHA, and so on. Also note, [3] the forms overall short code should be copied and pasted into your form management page, but more on that a little later. If we wanted to add a phone number field to this form as an example, we would click on the **Tel** button and fill in the descriptive information about the field, see Figure 5.12.

FIGURE 5.12

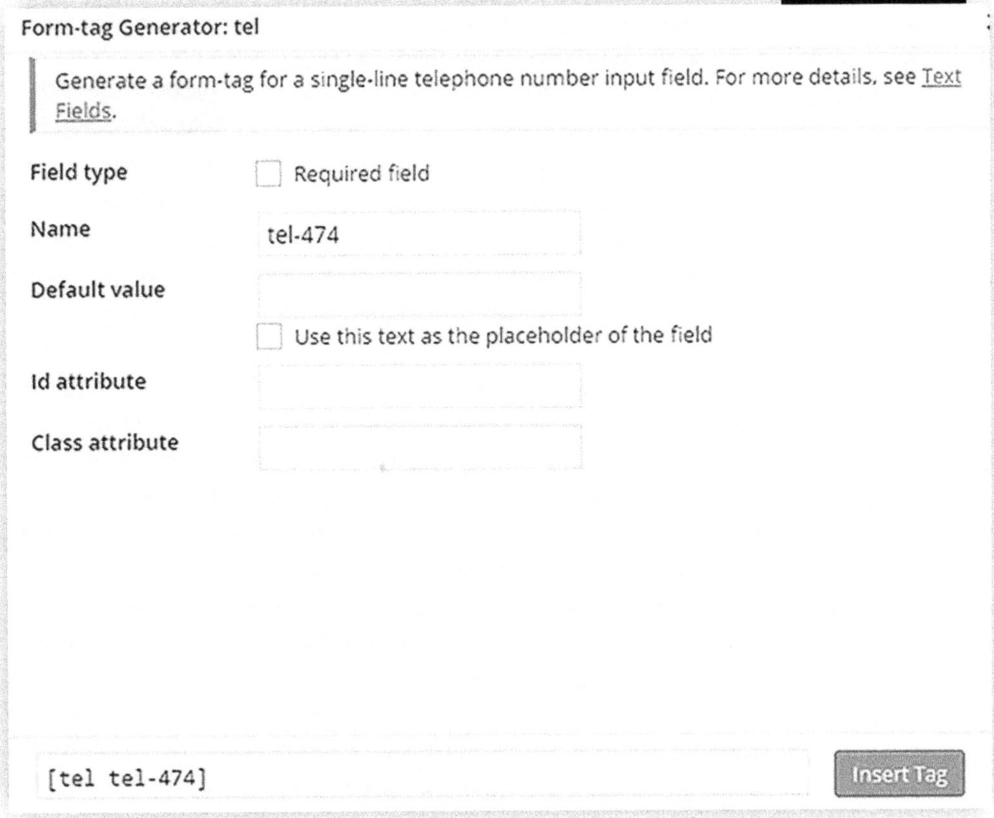

Here you can mark the field as required, give it a default value, and assigned the field custom CSS ID or class attributes. Note the newly created form field will be inserted at the location the cursor is sitting before you start the creation of a new field. This may affect your underlying form design, so it may be helpful to place your cursor before starting the process. You can always move the fields around later too, but you may find it easier to initially place the cursor where you want the new field created. The process of creating or editing a form also includes the elements descriptive text, so be sure to add that as well. The creation of a new form element via these buttons only creates the data entry area and not any supporting material such as descriptive text. Once you place the short code in a page and display the page you will be better able to adjust the design layout as you will be able to see what the form actually looks like.

The tabs along the top of the form designer have special functionality. *Contact Form 7* will send an email to a provided email address when a site visitor fills out and submits a form. The mail tab helps with these settings. Looking at Figure 5.13 you can see where you add in the email address which will receive the submitted form, who it's from, the subject of the form (copied from the form itself), who you can reply to (the sender's email address), and the message body. You can also see more of the additional information which can be added to the email; it's helpful data to see, especially if you have similar forms on multiple websites.

FIGURE 5.13

| Form | Mail | Messages | Additional Settings |

Mail

In the following fields, you can use these mail-tags:
`[your-name] [your-email] [your-subject] [your-message]`

To
`pbmacintyre@gmail.com`

From
`[your-name] <wordpress@testing.paladin-bs.com>`

Subject
`[your-subject]`

Additional Headers
`Reply-To: [your-email]`

Message Body
```
From: [your-name] <[your-email]>
Subject: [your-subject]

Message Body:
[your-message]

--
This e-mail was sent from a contact form on testing (http://testing.paladin-bs.com)
```

FIGURE 5.14

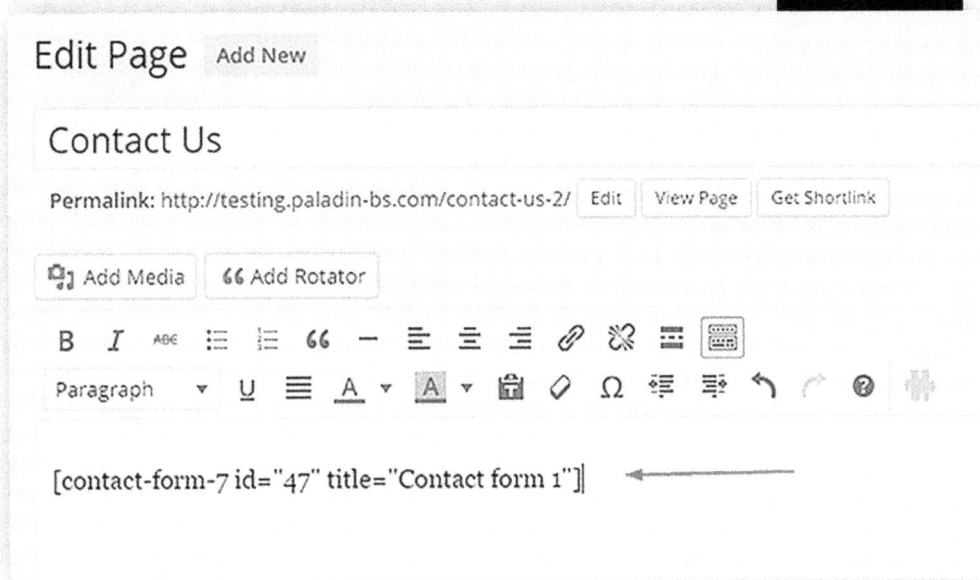

The messages tab allows you to be responsive to the site visitor by giving preset notes in reaction to the form being submitted. Different situations can occur like not filling in a required field and you can set response messages here to assist the person trying to fill in your form. The additional settings tab is another way to further fine-tune how your form behaves; there is a link on this tab which gives detailed help on what options are available to you, so be sure to explore those options.

Adding the overall forms short tag (after you have saved it, of course) to the desired page and then adding the page to the menu system will display in the form. Figure 5.14 shows the short tag being added to a page.

Figure 5.15 shows the form being displayed on the public site after clicking send on the entry form. This was done to show the messages which can be associated with the form.

FIGURE 5.15

Figure 5.16 shows the generated email *Contact Form 7* creates and sends.

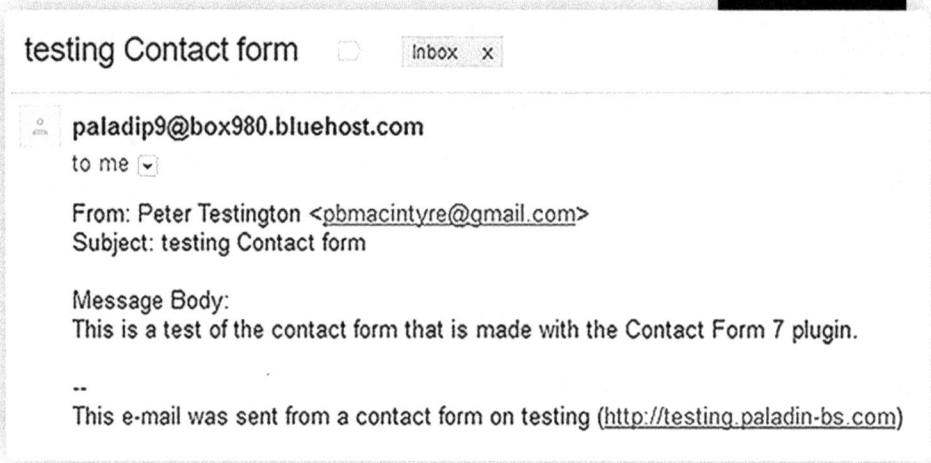

FIGURE 5.16

You are probably already ahead of the curve here on thinking about the data management issue. *Contact Form 7* leads to asking: "What if I want to retain the information submitted via a form in a data format rather than only having it sent to me in email?"

Enter *Contact Form DB*[4]. Simply install and activate this additional plugin and you will see *Contact Form DB* added to the admin menu. Click on this to show the data display page. In Figure 5.17 you will see a way to switch between different forms you may have active on your site [1], the listing of all the form submissions that have come in to date [2] with option to look at the details of the line items, and a mechanism to export the collected data [3] anytime you wish.

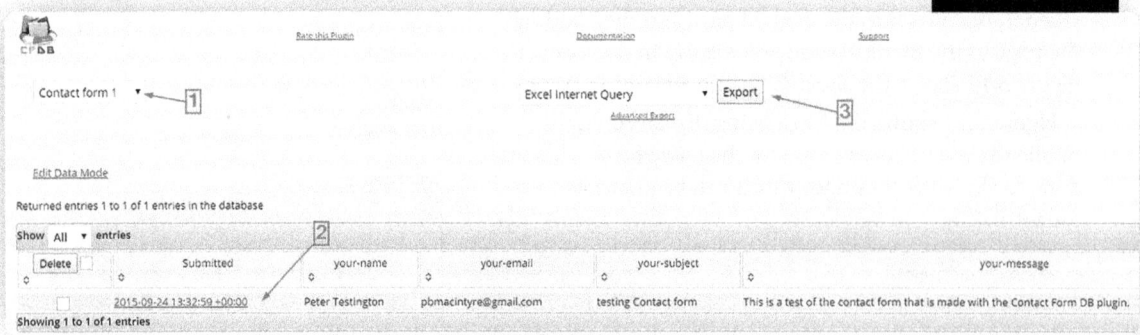

FIGURE 5.17

[4]   *Contact Form DB:* *https://wordpress.org/plugins/contact-form-7-to-database-extension/*

There is a great additional feature to this plugin which will also display the submitted form data in a generated short code. **Contact Form DB > Short Code** takes you to a short code builder page. In Figure 5.18 you can select the form data in question [1], select the output format you want [2], give the security level allowed to view this data (the master control of this is on the options page) [3], specify which form field you want to display (ignore this if you want them all) [4], select a sort order if desired [5], and then use the generated short code [6]. You can click directly on the short code if you want to see the output right away or you can copy the short code to a page and display the results that way.

FIGURE 5.18

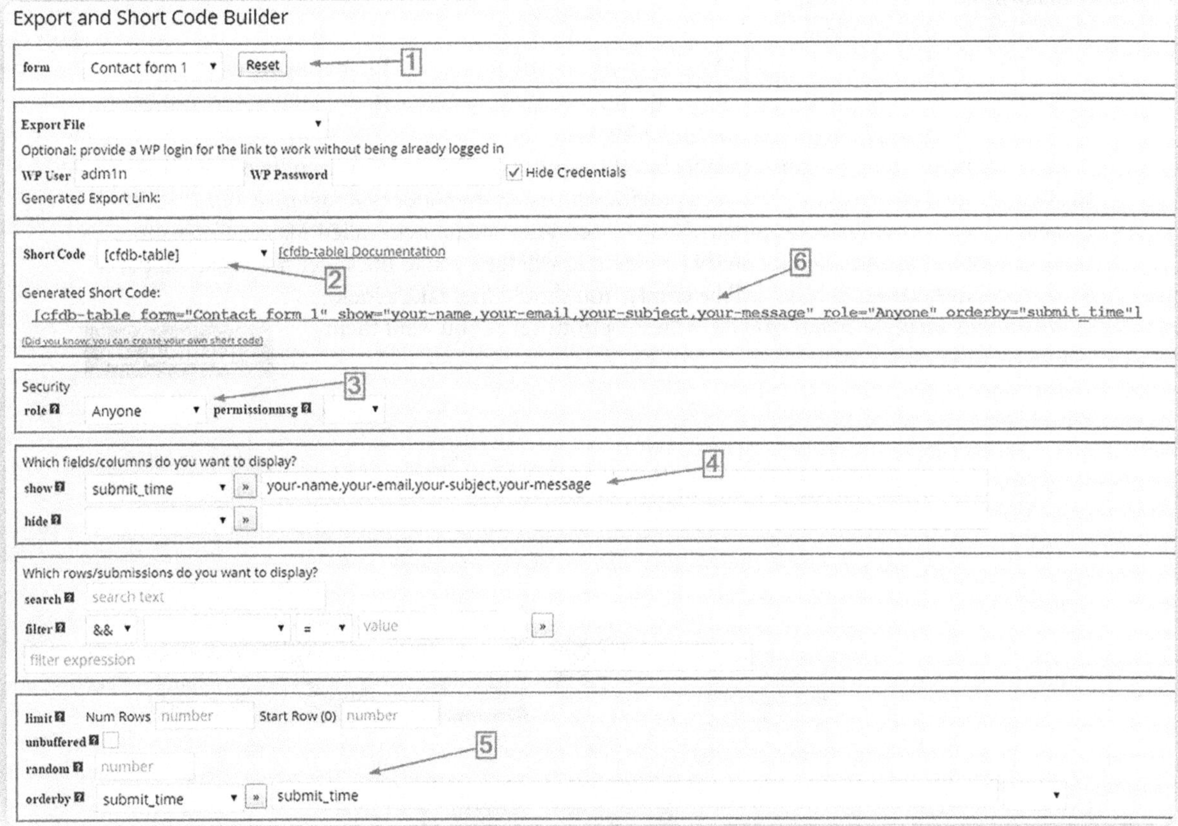

FIGURE 5.19

Of course, you will have to consider the security options of where and how you display this information. For demonstration purposes we are showing it on the public site in figure 5.19.

Data table

by ADMIN *on* SEPTEMBER 24, 2015

your-name	your-email	your-subject	your-message
Peter Testington	pbmacintyre@gmail.com	testing Contact form	This is a test of the contact form that is made with the Contact Form DB plugin.

Master Slider

Many modern websites use slider images. Although some may argue this design trend is on the wane, there are still many uses for an image slider that may not include a home page. You may want to show images from a recent conference you have attended, a birthday party, or a new product lineup.

There are many slider plugins available but the most versatile and user-friendly one we like the best is called *Master Slider*[5]. It's full plugin name is: *Master Slider - Responsive Touch Slider*. Locate, install, and activate this plugin. You will see a new menu item called *Master Slider* show up on the admin menu. Clicking on this menu item will take you to the slider management page. After initial installation, this list will be empty. You should first take a look at the settings menu to ensure you have these options set as you want them before creating slides.

FIGURE 5.20

The settings page for the whole plugin is quite sparse. This is by design since each slider you create can be specifically controlled on an individual basis. Check out these plugin wide settings and then navigate to the creation of a new slider by clicking on **Create New Slider** in the master slider control area. The new slider creation page looks like the one shown in Figure 5.20.

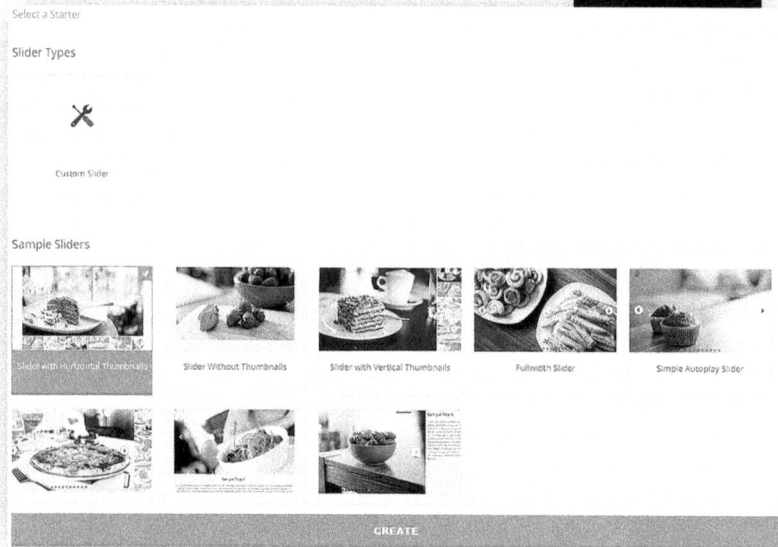

[5]   Master Slider: https://wordpress.org/plugins/master-slider/

Here you will be offered eight predefined styles of slider. Some have image previewing on the side, some on the bottom, some have no preview at all, and some will have areas for descriptive text for each individual image in the slider. Alternately, you can create a custom slider by choosing the similarly named button. For our example we will choose the first template called *slider with horizontal thumbnails*. To select a template, click on the sample and make sure it becomes highlighted; a blue check mark should also appear on the top right corner of the template. Click the large create button at the bottom of this page.

Once you select a template the plugin gives you 10 template sample images to start with. You can certainly replace these with your own images from your media library, but it's a great way to see what your slider will look like as you build it. Once you create a slider you will be taken to the slides area. Notice at the top of the page, see Figure 5.21, there are three other tabs which are part of the overall slider design.

Note the sample images are automatically added to your media library. If you do not want these sample images on your server, be sure to delete them from the media library.

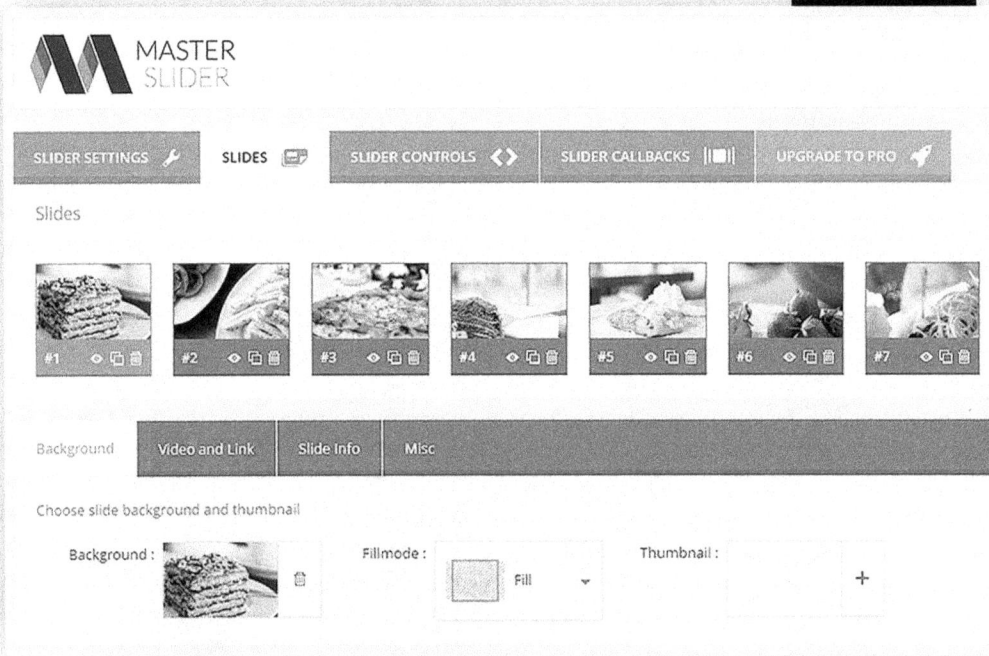

FIGURE 5.21

There is also a promotional tab enticing you to upgrade to the commercial version of the plugin. Before you start altering the slider images check on the slider settings and review some of the options there. The first thing you'll want to do is name the slide deck something meaningful to you. We have named the sample one "my first slider". Also take note of the navigation section here. You may want to ensure auto play and loop navigation are both turned on so your slide show starts when the page loads and will recycle when the last image is reached. Review the other settings on this page and adjust them to your desires be sure to save often or at least preview your changes.

Of important note, at the bottom of the slider settings page you will see an area called "short code" and in our case the short code is:

```
[masterslider id=1]
```

This is the short code you will use to place the completed slide deck elsewhere on your site. We are simply going to create a new page in our testing site and add it to the menu for display purposes. Otherwise, you would place this short code somewhere on a home page if you wanted the slider to be part of a site landing experience. Figure 5.22 shows the slider as added to the testing site.

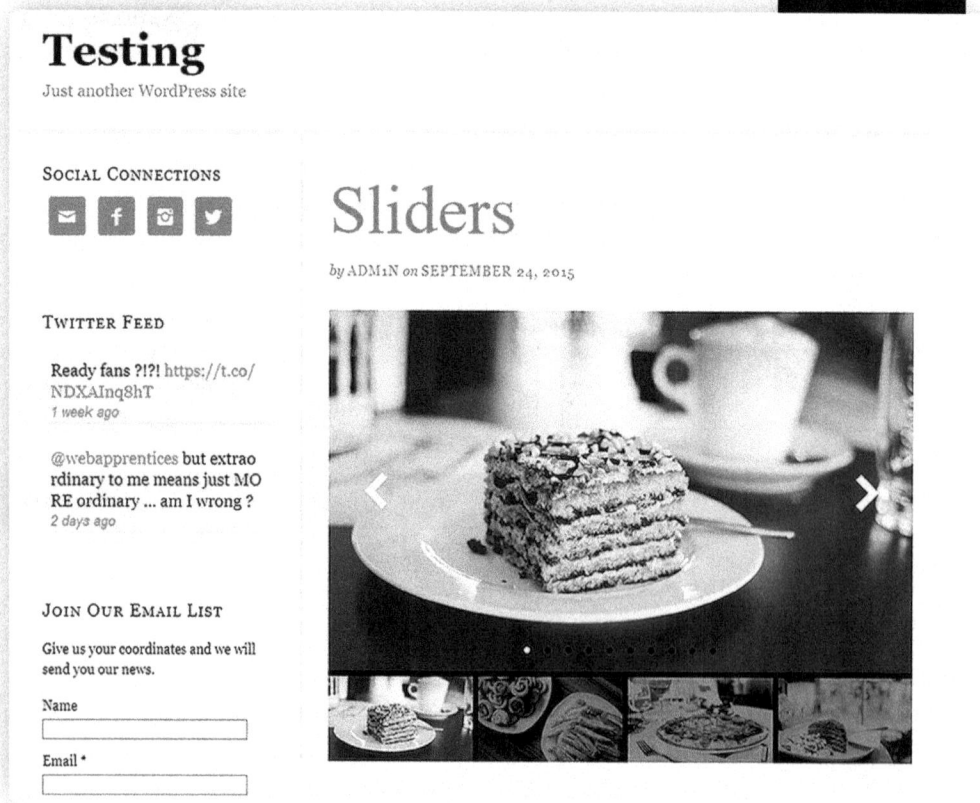

FIGURE 5.22

Getting back to the slider tab (Figure 5.21) you can see the images can be dragged to alter their order. You can delete slides and alter how they appear with the *Fill Mode* option. One of the features of this plugin which helps make it rise to the top of the heap is its ability to also include video links as part of the slide sequence. If you click on the *video and link* sub tab you will be shown the form fields to fill in with particular video information. On the slide info tab you can add text which will show if you have picked a slide template that shows additional text. And the *Misc* tab allows you to adjust slide specific CSS and change some of the color scheme on a slide-by-slide basis. The granularity of control on each slide is another large plus for this plugin. Under the *Slider Controls* tab you can alter what controls appear on the slider for slide navigation and timer appearances. For example, you can have the slider's left and right navigation arrows hide from view when the mouse pointer leaves the slider area. This can be a nice design option.

> NOTE: *another image presenting plugin that you may want to consider is one called* Huge IT Image Gallery. *It is well employed if you want a good image gallery as opposed to an image slider.*

WooCommerce

Do you want to sell anything online in a WordPress site? There are a few good ecommerce plugins on the market and there are some great commercial plugins as well. Since we are trying to build our WordPress sites with free plugins when we can, an excellent ecommerce plugin to discuss here is *WooCommerce*[6]. As you can imagine this is a large and involved plugin with many nuances to make online selling available to you.

Locate, install, and activate this plugin–you may be given the option of walking through a setup wizard, so make up your own mind about that (valuable to first time users, for sure). The value in the setup wizard is it will setup your shopping cart, your online shop, your check out, and your account pages for you. This alone can be a great time saver, so it is recommended you use this wizard. Other steps in the wizard help you:

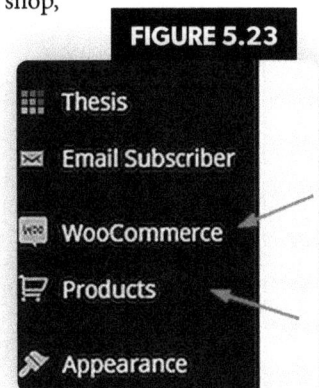

FIGURE 5.23

- set up your store location so it will then try to select a currency for you;
- set up your shipping and taxes;
- and setup your payment methods like PayPal, Bank Transfers, checks and so on.

Eventually, you will see a few menu items added to the admin menu, *WooCommerce* and *Products*.

[6]   WooCommerce: https://wordpress.org/plugins/woocommerce/

NOTE: *In order for you to have WooCommerce work with Thesis you have to purchase the WooCommerce Thesis Integrator plugin. This is a commercial plugin which currently costs $49.00 US. Visit the following link to register an account and to purchase the plugin: http://woocommerce-thesis-integration.com. There is a good video tutorial there as well which shows you how to install and setup the plugin properly. It guides you through the changes you have to make in the Skin Editor also.*

If you don't want to purchase this plugin you can also switch themes to one WooCommerce suggests called Storefront, but you would lose all the power and flexibility of Thesis. From this point on we will assume you have this plugin installed and working properly.

The first thing you would likely do is to add a product to your inventory: select **Products** > **Add Product**. The top portion of this interface should look familiar to you as it is closely related to a page or post creation. You should also see an area called *Product Data*, this may be further down the page so be sure to look for it. We have moved it up in our display so you can see it all in one screen image. Refer to Figure 5.24 to see the entry of our sample product called *Widget 11* [1]. We have provided a description [2]. You will want to identify whether or not the product is a physical item which will be shipped or something which is virtual (like a web video) [3]. You will also want to add in the SKU (Stock Keeping Unit) and pricing [4] for the product.

FIGURE 5.24

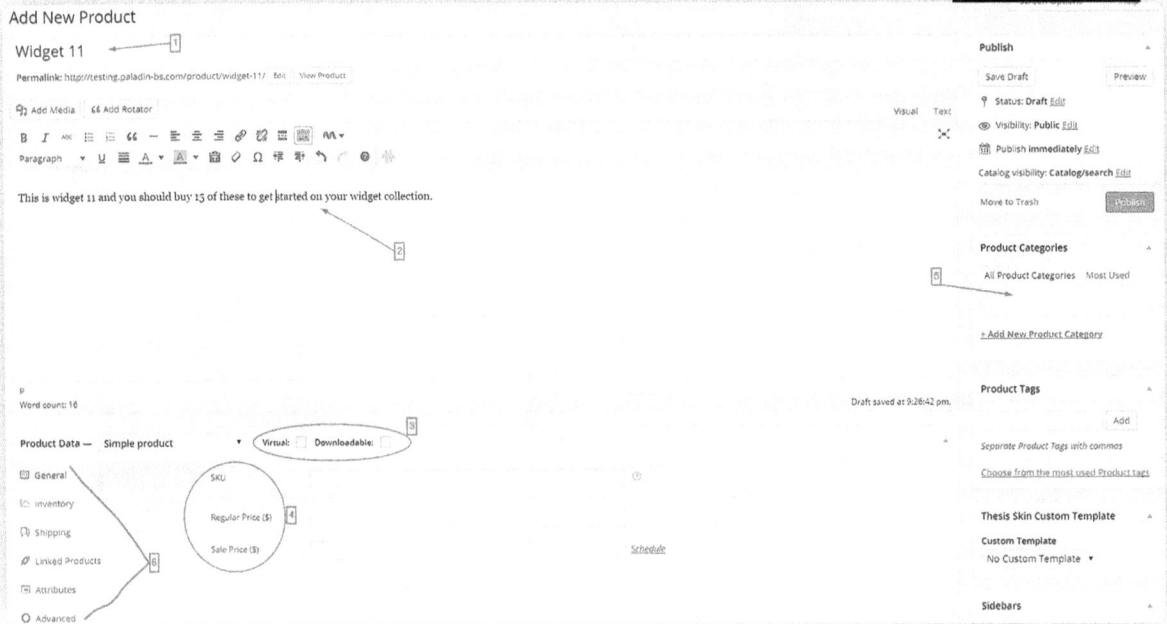

In addition to naming the product you can also put it into a category [5] you create and maintain, this could help organize your online store if you are going to have a large inventory so customers can find products easily. You can direct your online shop to handle and organize these categories as well. Under the *Product Data* section you will also see vertical tabs [6] in which you can further manage your individual product details. If you select the *Inventory* tab for example, you can control the product thresholds (stock on hand, allowance for back ordering, and so on) if the product is a physical item. The shipping tab allows you to set the product's weight for calculating the shipping fees, Linked Products allows you to offer upselling ("This other product has a better warranty") or cross selling ("People that bought this item also bought this item").

Additionally, you should add a product image and make a decision on if you want to allow customer feedback on your products. All these options are available on the individual product creation page.

NOTE: WooCommerce and Thesis create page templates for you to use as part of the installation setup wizard of WooCommerce. Figure 5.25 shows the Thesis Skin Editor menu with the Product page open and other pages available on the list like Refunds, Coupons, and Order. This means you can design your pages of your ecommerce site to look exactly as you want them too, and they can be individually designed as well. Also, if you have followed the guide to the additional integration plugin you should be well setup within the skin editor and ready to open your shop.

FIGURE 5.25

Naturally, you will have to add these new pages to your menu system so your site visitors can see what you have on offer. We have added two widgets to the products list and added the Shop and Cart Pages to the site menu. Figure 5.26 shows the Shop page and Figure 5.27 shows the Cart page. With CSS you can alter the colors of the action buttons and the other colors of WooCommerce, so if you don't like the default purple you can certainly change it to match your design.

There are other pages and features you can setup and show within WooCommerce like allowing your customers to open accounts so they can save their addresses for future purchases and so on. For now, we will just focus on the financial aspect of the plugin.

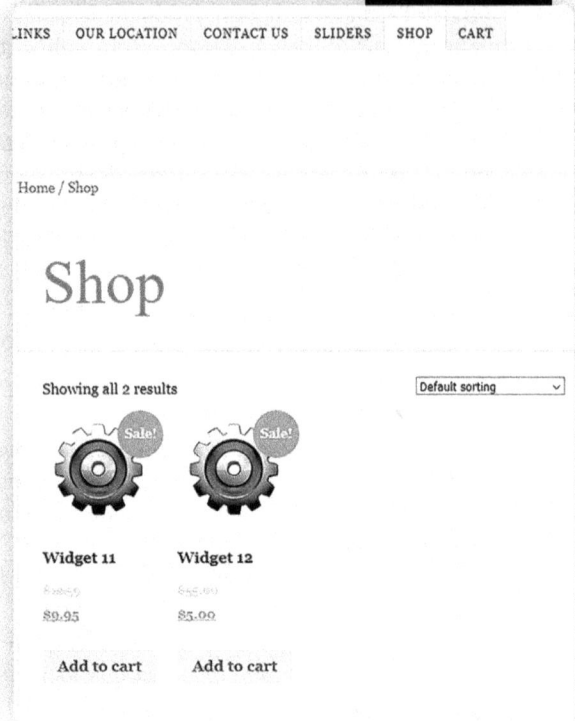

FIGURE 5.26

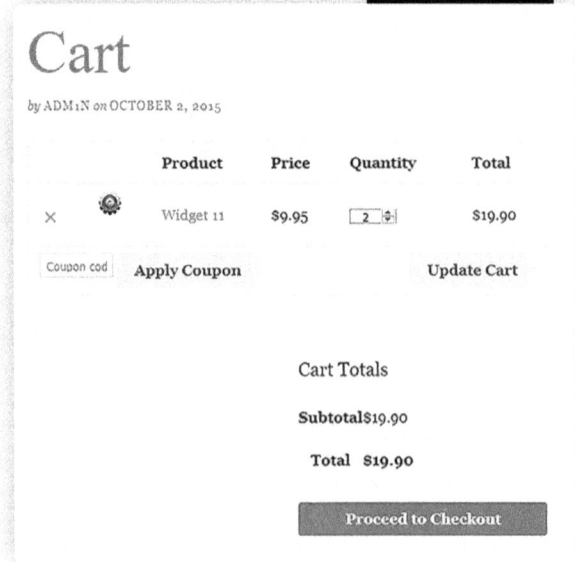

FIGURE 5.27

In order to receive money from your customers you will need a connection to a financial service like PayPal, Stripe, BACS (Direct wire transfers), etc. WooCommerce comes with a connection to PayPal for simple transactions (PayPal Standard), all the other integration points need to be purchased and setup. PayPal Standard is good enough to get started in the ecommerce world. Once properly setup, it will take you to a PayPal screen outside your site and allows the customer to pay with PayPal funds or with a credit card. This has the benefit of your site not needing to be cryptographically secured with an SSL certificate or the responsibility of handling and storing your customers' credit card numbers. To see where you would setup the financial integration you should follow this menu path: **WooCommerce > Settings > Checkout (tab)** then under the *Checkout* tab select PayPal. Figure 5.28 shows this setup page.

FIGURE 5.28

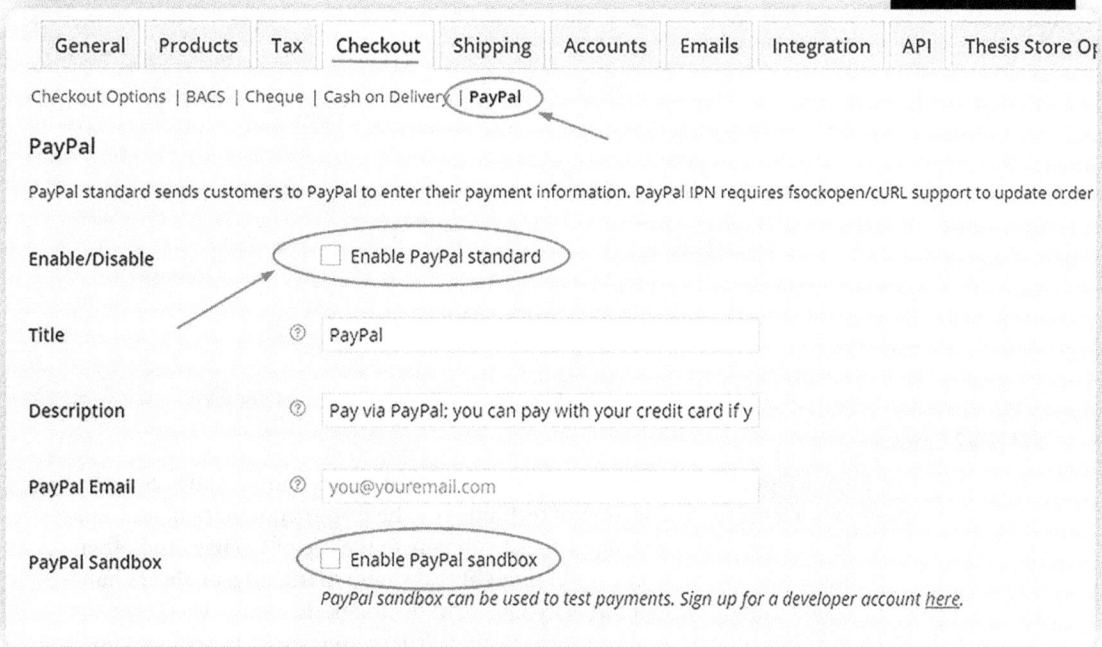

Notice here that you would have to turn on (enable) PayPal Standard or you can also enable their "Sandbox" testing account here as well. The sandbox feature is great for use with a developer account where you can test all of the aspects of PayPal integration without having to move real money around as you build your ecommerce site.

WooCommerce does come with many additional add-ons you may want to consider. You may want to use a different financial conduit like Stripe, have a UPS or FedEx shipping option to offer your customers and so on. If you click on **WooCommerce > Add-ons** you will see a summary of some of the more common add-ons you may want to implement. Keep in mind many of these are paid add-ons so be sure you will get your ROI for them. For a full listing of all currently available add-ons (currently there are over 350 of them); visit woothemes[7].

WooCommerce is a versatile plugin and we can't cover every usage scenario it is capable of handling. Due to space and scope constraints we will have to leave it here. But, before we leave we want to highlight a few more key features. Be sure to explore the coupons area, the reports area, and the shipping setup area (if you are dealing with physical products). WooCommerce also adds a summary area to the WordPress Dashboard which gives you a quick overview of your current ecommerce transactions. This is shown in Figure 5.29. Here you are shown an overview of your orders and any stock level warnings that may need your attention.

FIGURE 5.29

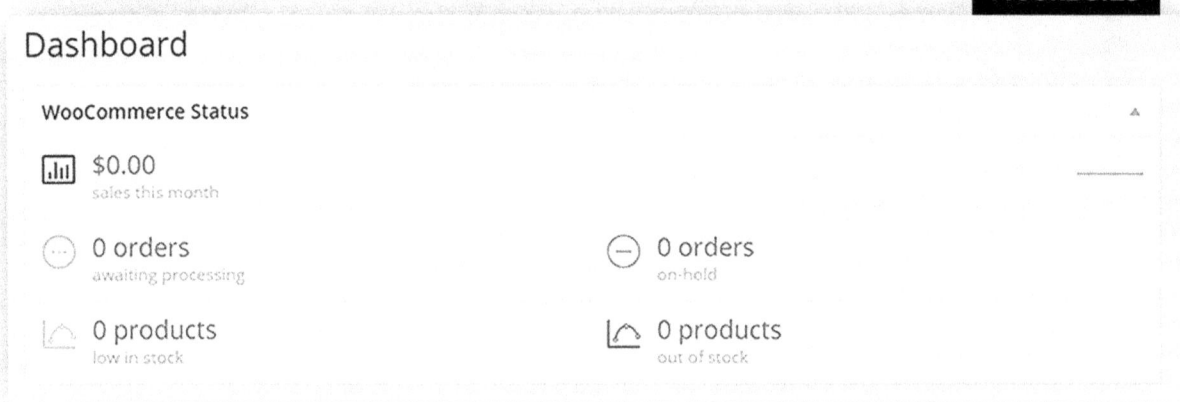

Yoast SEO

SEO or Search Engine Optimization is a science in and of itself. As its name implies, Search Engine Optimization is a term for a collection of techniques to help your content rank and show up higher in search engine results. The struggle to get your site to the top of Google (and other engines) search results is one which takes careful thought and sound marketing, or sheer chance and good luck. It's a good thing to attempt to get your site to the top of the search list. Enter the *Yoast SEO*[8] plugin. This plugin helps you with specifically targeting your SEO content on granular level. It even lets you set up SEO content on a page by page level and offers you some helpful tips along the way.

Locate the plugin install and activate it as you would with any other WordPress plugin. You should see a new menu item on the admin menu simply called "SEO". If you click on **SEO > General** immediately after your install finishes you will see some helpful tips and any major SEO issues your site currently has. Figure 5.30 shows an example of this.

[7]   woothemes: http://phpa.me/woocommerce-ext
[8]   Yoast SEO: https://wordpress.org/plugins/wordpress-seo/

FIGURE 5.30

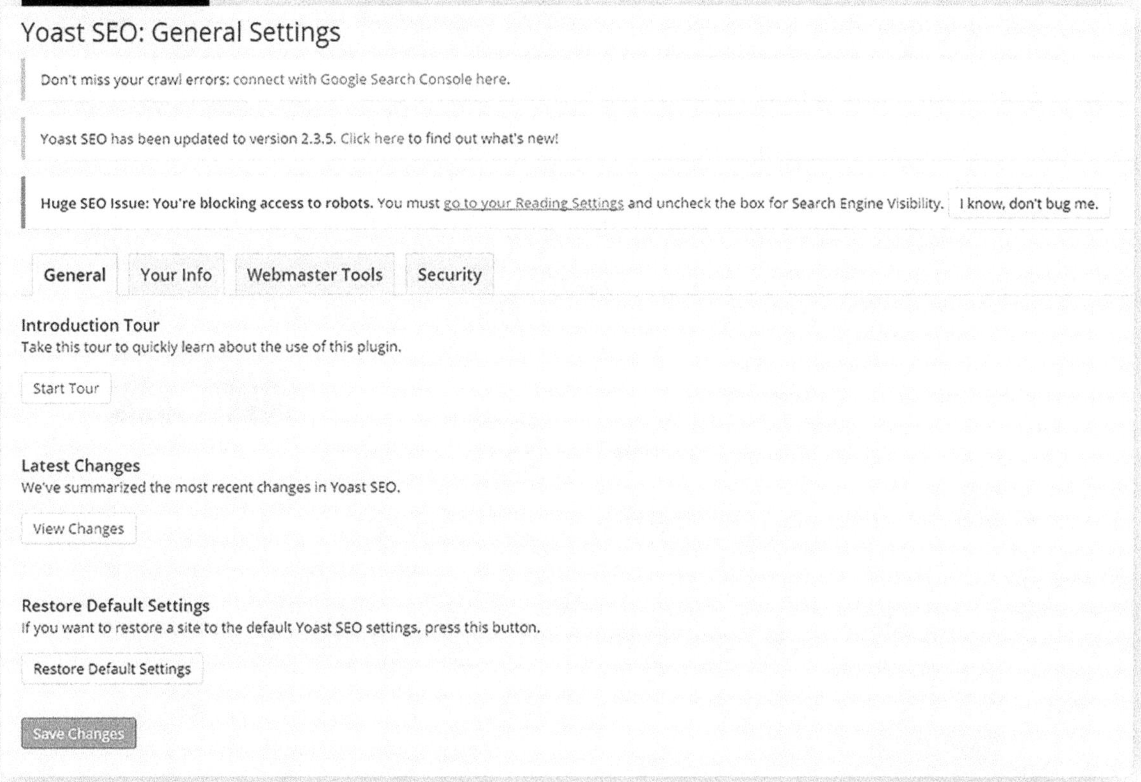

Yoast SEO: General Settings

Don't miss your crawl errors: connect with Google Search Console here.

Yoast SEO has been updated to version 2.3.5. Click here to find out what's new!

Huge SEO Issue: You're blocking access to robots. You must go to your Reading Settings and uncheck the box for Search Engine Visibility.   I know, don't bug me.

| General | Your Info | Webmaster Tools | Security |

Introduction Tour
Take this tour to quickly learn about the use of this plugin.

Start Tour

Latest Changes
We've summarized the most recent changes in Yoast SEO.

View Changes

Restore Default Settings
If you want to restore a site to the default Yoast SEO settings, press this button.

Restore Default Settings

Save Changes

NOTE: *Take a look at this guide if you are completely new to SEO concepts: http://phpa.me/google-webmasters-seo-starter-guide. Yoast has its own guide as well: https://yoast.com/wordpress-seo/. The more information you can get on this topic will just make your site that much better and easier to find, so do read these and do some of your own research online as well.*

To add SEO content on a site wide basis you should start on the *Your Info* tab **SEO > General > Your Info**. Here you simply add some generic content about your site like its name and whether or not your site is for personal or commercial use. The next area you want to look at is accessed here: **SEO > Titles & Metas**. There are a at least two tabs of interest here: namely, *Homepage* and *Post Types*. On the *Homepage* tab, SEO offers you a page title template you should verify and a place to add your Meta description. This description should be written with a site-wide perspective in mind. Choose your words carefully and be concise, this content will appear on your homepage and will be collected by the search engines when they visit and index your site. It will help search engine users by introducing them to your site.

The other tab of special interest here is the *Post Types* tab. Here you can set up templates for SEO content which will appear by default on all your pages, posts, media, and so on. This is very important to do if you don't plan on (or have the time) to target your SEO content on a unique page by page basis. This allows you to set something custom to appear when you create new posts or pages and so on. Figure 5.31 shows this template page being filled in. The *Meta Robots* setting adds some markup to the page to tell well-behaved search engine robots and spiders if they should index your page's content and follow links in the page. *Date in Snippet Preview* adds the date the page or post was published to the rich snippet serving as a description. *Yoast SEO Meta Box* controls if the Meta Box plugin will be displayed on the edit form. You'll have to do some research to decide if any should be enabled for your site, but in the beginning it's safe to stick with the defaults.

FIGURE 5.31

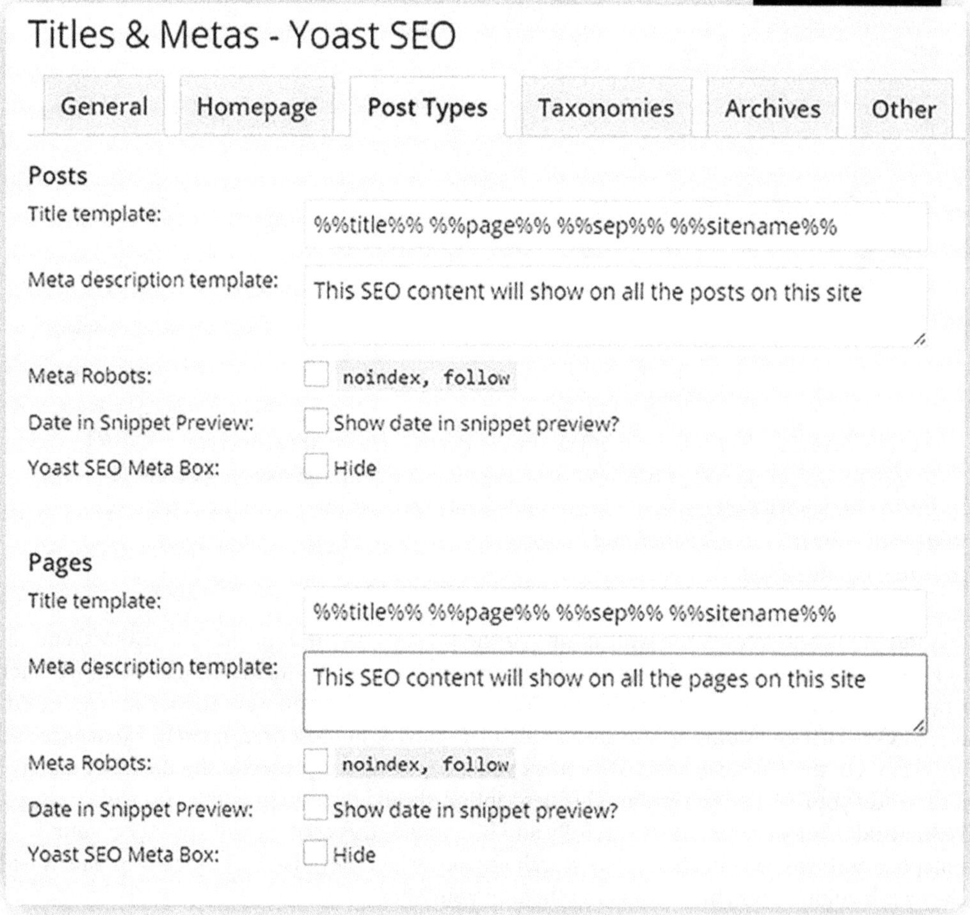

Titles & Metas - Yoast SEO

| General | Homepage | Post Types | Taxonomies | Archives | Other |

Posts

Title template:
`%%title%% %%page%% %%sep%% %%sitename%%`

Meta description template:
This SEO content will show on all the posts on this site

Meta Robots: ☐ noindex, follow

Date in Snippet Preview: ☐ Show date in snippet preview?

Yoast SEO Meta Box: ☐ Hide

Pages

Title template:
`%%title%% %%page%% %%sep%% %%sitename%%`

Meta description template:
This SEO content will show on all the pages on this site

Meta Robots: ☐ noindex, follow

Date in Snippet Preview: ☐ Show date in snippet preview?

Yoast SEO Meta Box: ☐ Hide

The real power in this plugin though is in how it manages the SEO content on a page by page or post by post basis. If you look at any page in the page management area (we are looking at our *Sample Page* here), you will see a new section called *Yoast SEO*. Here you can add your SEO content specifically targeted to the content of this page. Once you add some of the content the SEO plugin will analyze what you have entered and provide a summary for you under the *Focus Keyword* section. As shown in Figure 5.32, you can see the keyword *Sample* is well represented in all areas except for the text content of the page itself. Also note when you add in your meta description the plugin builds a *Snippet Preview*—this is what the page will likely look like when it is found and displayed on a Google search result. You can see just how important your SEO content can be.

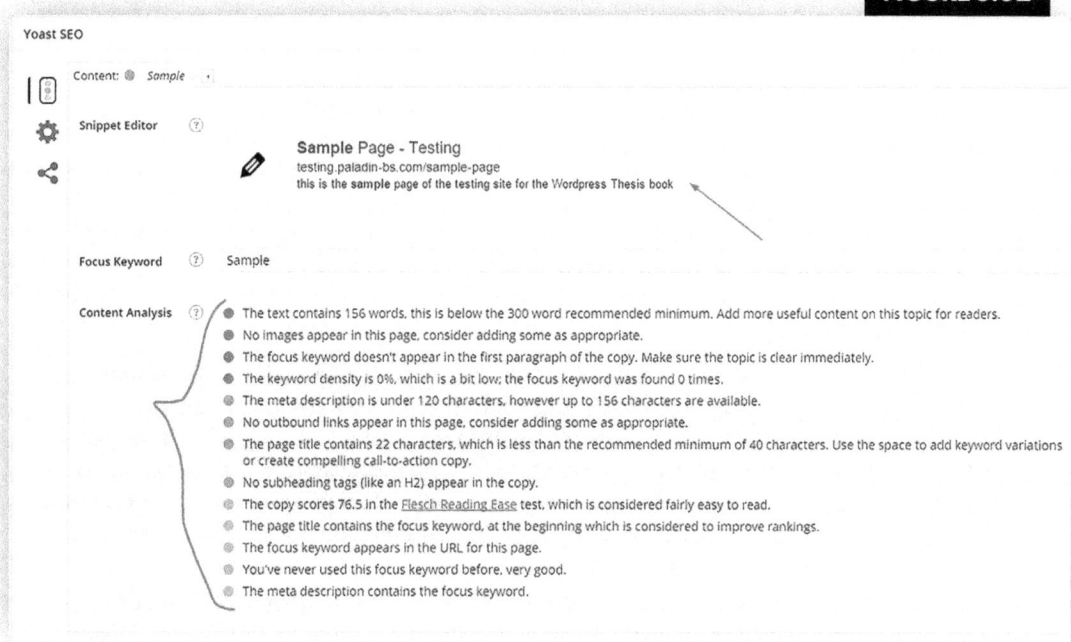

FIGURE 5.32

Also shown in Figure 5.32, you can see a deep review of the content of this particular page with color coding on the information that is given back. The analysis also reports on some of the good things you have going for you from the SEO point of view. This feedback can really help to make your site more prominent on the web so be sure to use this plugin to its full potential.

On the left side of this area are two vertical tab items: a gear and three connected circles. The gear area is where you can add your SEO meta tag content specific to the page or post that you are editing. The tab area of the three connected circles is where you can make connections to both Facebook and Twitter. Figure 5.33 shows the Twitter connection area. The premium edition of this plugin has areas for many more social media connections.

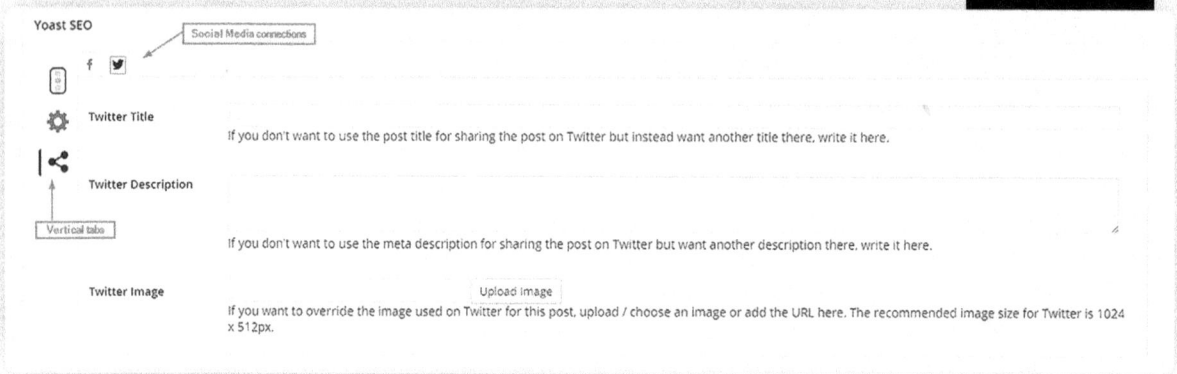

FIGURE 5.33

WP eMember ($)

The next major plugin we will be looking at here is one called *WP eMember*[9]. If you want to control content on your website and have different levels of access, free members, and paid members (or multiple levels) then this is the plugin of choice. Install this plugin by the upload method once you have purchased it and downloaded it to your local system. This is a commercial plugin which can be purchased. Its current price is $59.95 US. If you scroll to the bottom of the page, you will see a list of free add-ons. The Captcha and Email Broadcast add-ons are two of the more valuable ones.

WP eMember will be added to your admin menu. Click on **WP eMember** > **Dashboard** to see the basic settings tabs called *Dashboard, Members, Membership Levels*, and *Settings*. However, before you get into changing too much information you should take some time to plan what types of memberships you want to offer and how many levels you want to have for your site visitors. A basic setup would be to have most of your site with free access and certain other pages set aside for paid memberships. You can control most of these settings and preferences by clicking on the *Settings* menu item. Here, shown in Figure 5.34, you can see six or seven tabs depending on the number of additional add-on plugins you have. The first tab, *General Settings*, is where you select your language and make some basic decisions. If, for example, you are going to have a free membership level which still requires site visitors to sign in (essentially another level of membership), then you need to create this membership level here **WP eMember** > **Membership**

[9]   *WP eMember:* https://www.tipsandtricks-hq.com/?p=1706

Level and keep the membership level number that is created (#1 if it is your first level created in the system), check this box and then also provide the level number on this page. If you scroll down on the general settings tab you will see a vast amount of settings available. Take some time to review these options and plan your memberships well.

FIGURE 5.34

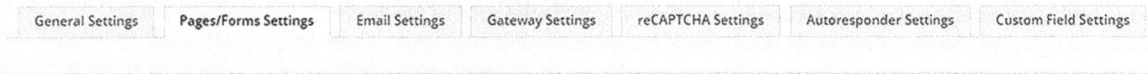

WP eMembers - Settings v8.9.4

| General Settings | Pages/Forms Settings | Email Settings | Gateway Settings | reCAPTCHA Settings | Autoresponder Settings | Custom Field Settings |

The *Pages/Forms Settings* tab is the place to control what happens when events occur. For example, you may want to direct a member to a certain page after they login or logout. Some of these pages are created for you in default format when you first install the plugin. Be sure to check out these pages and season them to your own tastes or create new ones and put their URL path in the appropriate location for your desired action.

The *Email Settings* tab is where you control the content of generated emails when a new member signs up to your site or other events which might happen to a member. There are eight email generating scenarios, so the control over what is said to your members in these situations is a very nice feature. There are even emails which can be sent out for a membership which is about to expire (reminder to renew) to help maintain your members list.

The *Gateway Settings* tab is where you set up your connection to a payment processing engine such as PayPal. Here you connect to a payment button you create in your PayPal interface for use on your site. After you create the button in PayPal you are provided with a code block you copy into your web page. When a member is trying to pay you for joining one of your paid memberships you can have them click on this PayPal button and all the financial aspects will be taken care of by PayPal.

Once the settings are all tailored to your needs, you can then control which membership level can see certain content on your site. On your Pages and Posts edit forms (and any other place *WP eMember* can control) you will see a new section called *eMember Protection Options*. Shown in Figure 5.35, you can see the content on this page is now protected and only those members whose level is *Gold* can see it.

FIGURE 5.35

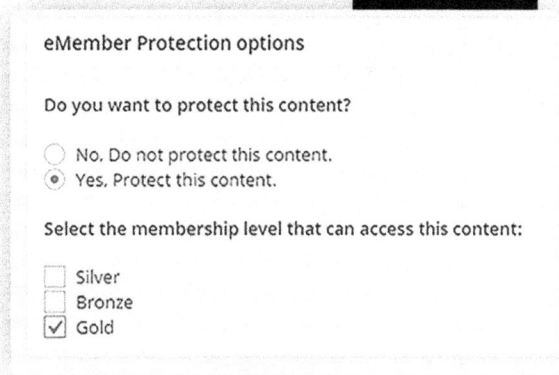

eMember Protection options

Do you want to protect this content?

◯ No. Do not protect this content.
◉ Yes. Protect this content.

Select the membership level that can access this content:

☐ Silver
☐ Bronze
☑ Gold

Backup Scheduler

Naturally, once you have your website all constructed exactly how you want it, you will want to have peace of mind with a backup of the site. *Backup Scheduler*[10] is the plugin we use for this (and there are many backup tools and plugins to be sure). We find this to be among the best and the easiest to use.

As its name implies, this is a plugin which allows you to set a schedule of what and when you want your site to be backed up. This is different than the plugin we looked at in Chapter Four called *WP Clone*. WP Clone can be used for backups, but they can only be done manually.

Install and activate this plugin and you should see a new admin menu item appear called *SL Plugins*. This is the parent item for the company that created and maintains the backup scheduler. To access the scheduler itself, follow this menu path: **SL Plugins > Backup Scheduler**. On this page you will see a few different tabs; the two of note are *Backups* (this lists the existing backups if there are any), and *Parameters* (where you set up your schedule). You should really begin with the parameters tab unless you are performing a "forced", or manual, backup. Figure 5.36 shows this screen before any scheduling is entered.

FIGURE 5.36

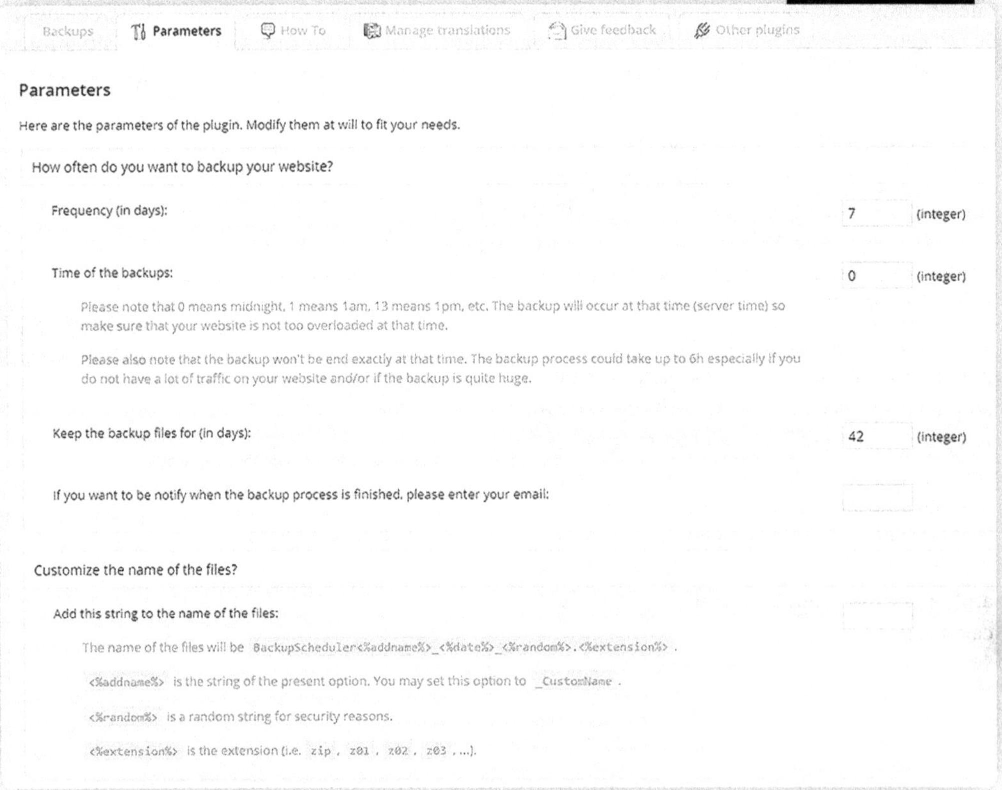

[10]   *Backup Scheduler: https://wordpress.org/plugins/backup-scheduler/*

Here you can set how often you want a scheduled backup to run with the frequency setting and the time of day you want the backup to run in 24-hour clock mode AKA—military time. It also allows you to set how many days you want to retain your backups. In addition, you can tell the plugin to email you when a backup is completed, if so desired. Last, you can customize the naming scheme of the backup file names.

One thing to keep in mind here is you are storing the backup files on the same server from which you are serving your site to the public. If the server should have a catastrophic failure, then your backups would be useless to you as well.

We also use an outside tool called *SyncBack*[11] which allows for a scheduled downloading of selected files (we do the entire site, which includes all the saved backups, each night with weekly and monthly instances) via FTP connections made within the SyncBack tool. This copies the files down to a local external hard drive, which can also fill up over time, so maybe as a long term backup solution you could either delete backups you no longer need, or burn them to a DVD disk for long term storage. Keep in mind DVDs are not forever and even they will deteriorate over long periods of time. If your information is invaluable, you should look into more secure long term backup media.

SyncBack is for Windows machines only, but there are similar tools for other operating systems. For Unix-like OSs, rsync is a popular tool for quickly copying files from one machine to another. See *http://phpa.me/do-rsync-copy* for more information.

If you are following a pattern similar to the one described above then you can tell *Backup Scheduler* to delete the saved backups from the server after maybe 5 days since you are downloading them to a separate location from your server anyway.

Inline Google Spreadsheet Viewer

The next great tool to consider using is *Inline Google Spreadsheet Viewer*[12], a plugin which imports data from a Google spreadsheet (and other formats like CSV files) into your site seamlessly. This is a great product because you can update the spreadsheet's data via the Google interface and later have your data displayed on your web page. After you install and activate the plugin you will see a menu item added to the settings menu: **Settings > Inline Google Spreadsheet Viewer**. Take a look at these settings if you need to adjust the source of the data you are importing or to change the CSS naming convention of the DataTable class. Generally, these options are fine in their default settings. The power in this plugin comes from its ability to be controlled by options added to the short code or by adjusting the CSS controlling the table layout.

[11] SyncBack: *http://www.2brightsparks.com/syncback/syncback-hub.html*
[12] Inline Google Spreadsheet Viewer: *https://wordpress.org/plugins/inline-google-spreadsheet-viewer/*

Once you have identified a Google sheet to use, be sure it is set to allow for viewing by the general public on Google. Figure 5.37 shows where this setting can be found once you open the sharing section of the Google sheet. This has to be set at this level of viewership so the plugin can access the data freely; be sure the data you want to display is not protected or sensitive.

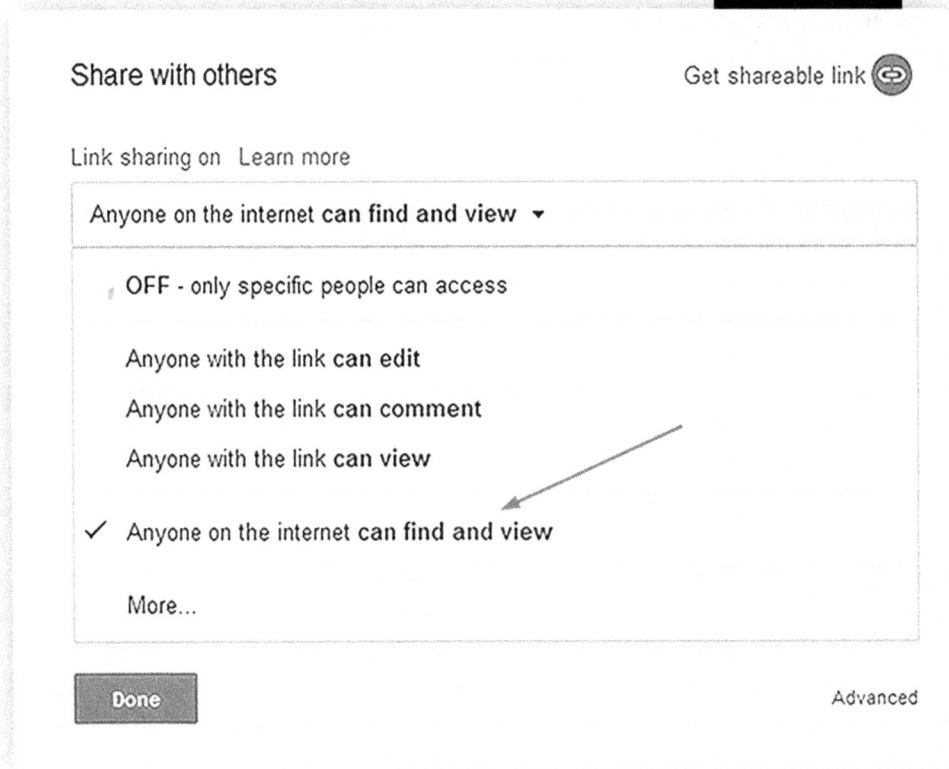

FIGURE 5.37

Once you have the sheet setup on Google simply copy the URL to the sheet and paste it into a WordPress page or post as part of the following short code (all on one line):

```
[gdoc key="https://docs.google com/spreadsheets/d/10M_KRZw6tDAURYJX25b_60UsMmFCKL1QS
6LwE8ZFsC4/edit?usp=sharing"]
```

"gdoc" is the beginning of the short code identifying the plugin being used and the "key" is the URL address for the shared page. Figure 5.38 shows the Google spreadsheet imported into our testing WordPress site in its raw state.

FIGURE 5.38

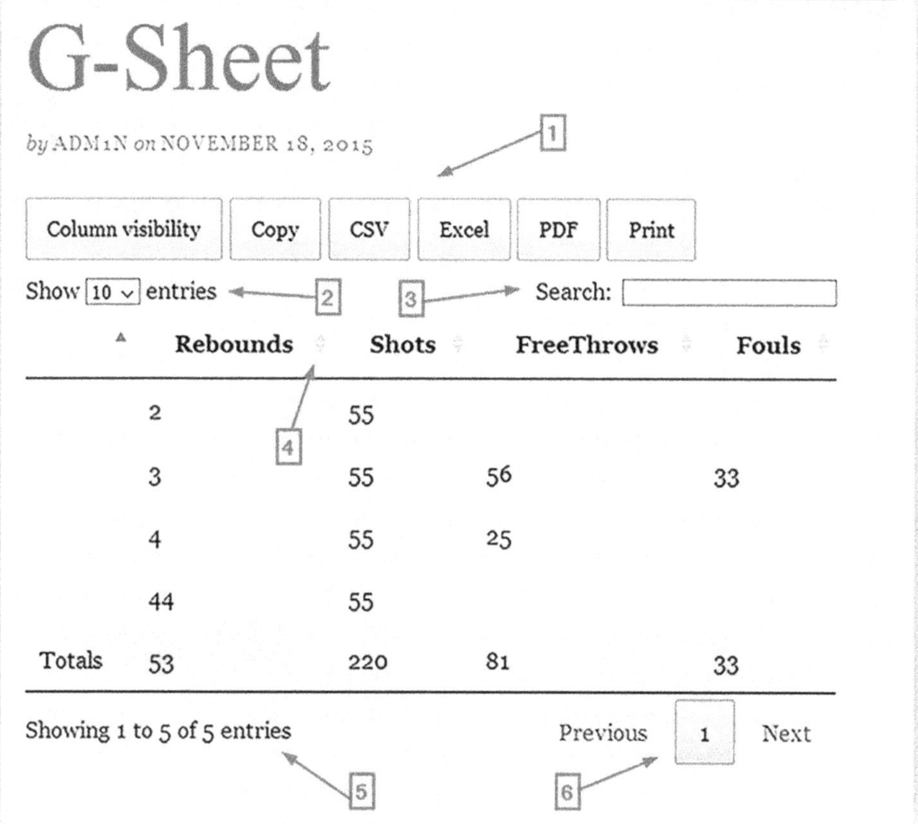

G-Sheet

by ADMIN *on* NOVEMBER 18, 2015

| Column visibility | Copy | CSV | Excel | PDF | Print |

Show 10 entries [2] [3] Search:

▲ Rebounds	Shots	FreeThrows	Fouls
2	55		
3	55	56	33
4	55	25	
44	55		
Totals 53	220	81	33

Showing 1 to 5 of 5 entries [5] [6] Previous | 1 | Next

[1] are the default export buttons the page viewer can use if they want to copy the data themselves; [2] is the option for the user to control how many rows of data to show at a time; [3] is a localized search feature for locating data on the sheet itself (not site wide); [4] are the controls for altering the sort order for each column in the table; [5] shows the summary of the table and how many rows are currently in view; [6] allows for pagination of the data in the sheet. All these options are controllable with either short code options or CSS statements.

In this example we want to display the table data only and not allow for all the options. The options in the short code to adjust the display are summarized in the table below.

Option	Description
use_cache="no"	Disables the caching of the data, allowing for the data to be imported from the Google source instantly (on page refresh). With caching on, the data is imported or refreshed every 10 minutes which may prove helpful if you are expecting high traffic to this page and the data will not be changing often.
datatables_searching="false"	Will remove the sheet's custom search tool [3]
datatables_ordering="false"	Will turn off the column sorting options [4]
dataTables_info="false"	Will turn off the summary display at the bottom of the table [5]
datatables_paging="false"	Will turn off the pagination on the display [6]

With all these options added to the short code it will look like this and display as shown in Figure 5.39

```
[gdoc key="https://docs.googl.com/spreadsheets/d/ \
10M_KRZw6tDAURYJX25b_60UsMmFCKL1QS6LwE8ZFsC4/edit?usp=sharing"
use_cache="no" datatables_paging="false" datatables_ordering="false"
datatables_searching="false" dataTables_info="false"]
```

FIGURE 5.39

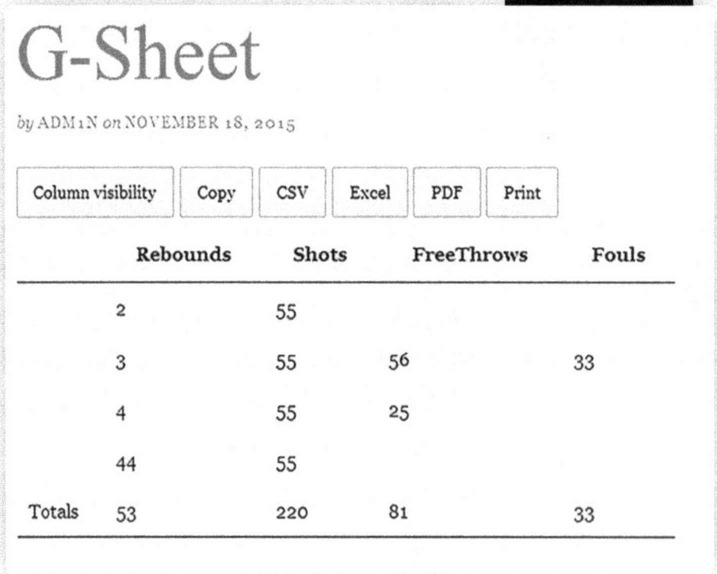

G-Sheet

by ADMIN *on* NOVEMBER 18, 2015

| Column visibility | Copy | CSV | Excel | PDF | Print |

	Rebounds	Shots	FreeThrows	Fouls
	2	55		
	3	55	56	33
	4	55	25	
	44	55		
Totals	53	220	81	33

NOTE: If you have multiple Google sheets (spreadsheet tabs) from the same Google spread-sheet you want to use on the same WordPress page, all you have to do is replicate the short code and update the full URL for each sheet.

As you can see, this display is much cleaner, but we are still not done with how this sheet can be styled. If you noticed in the settings page the default CSS class designation for this table is `igsv-table`. This can be used for the following styling of the table:

```css
/*==== Stats Sheet google sheet styling ==================*/

.igsv-table tr.odd {
    /* styles for odd-numbered rows   (row 1, 3, 5...) */
    background-color: red;
}
.igsv-table tr.even {
    /* styles for even-numbered rows   (row 2, 4, 6...) */
    background-color: #C6C6C6;
}

.row-1 th, .row-6 {
    background-color: #E0823F !important;
    text-align: center !important;
}
.col-2, .col-3, .col-4, .col-5, .col-6 {
    border-left: solid black 1px;
    text-align: right ;
}
.buttons-copy, .buttons-csv   {
    display: none !important;
}
```

Notice the CSS is being used to alter the color of the even rows in the table (the code is there for you to see for the odd rows as well, but we are not altering the display in this example). The CSS class name is being used here but we are also changing the display for the first and 6th rows of this table to make them appear as headers and footers; and we are changing the borders of the columns (`border-left`) so they can be differentiated from each other. We are even controlling the display of the buttons on the top of the table to hide some of the export options.

NOTE: The CSS names for all the buttons are:

- `.buttons-colvis` - Column Visibility
- `.buttons-copy` - Copy Button
- `.buttons-csv` - CSV Button
- `.buttons-excel` - Excel Button
- `.buttons-pdf` - PDF Button
- `.buttons-print` - Print Button

The displayed table now looks like Figure 5.40. There is a lot of help on the plugin's website for even more fine tuning if you are interested:
https://wordpress.org/plugins/inline-google-spreadsheet-viewer/faq/

FIGURE 5.40

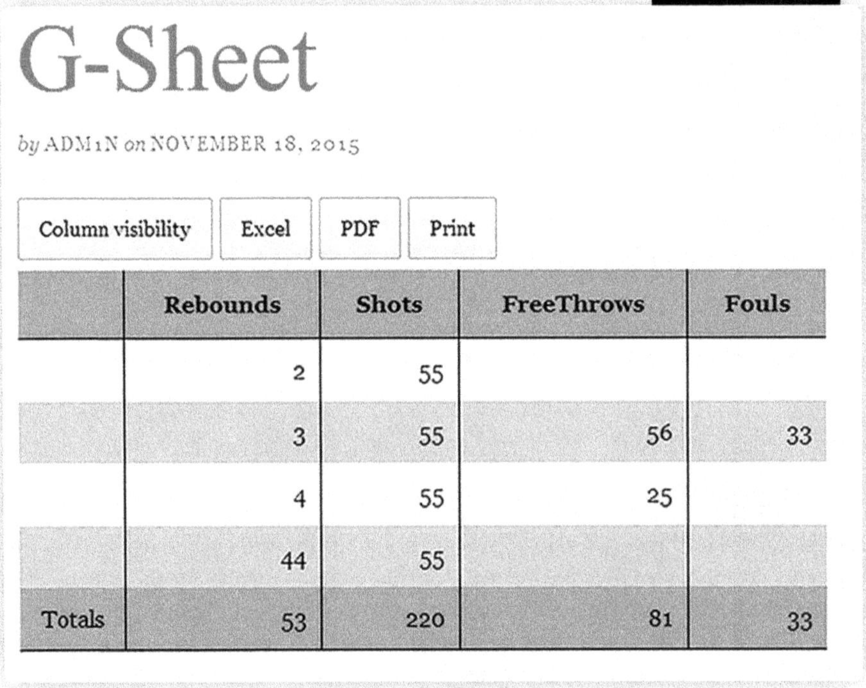

G-Sheet

by ADMIN *on* NOVEMBER 18, 2015

| Column visibility | Excel | PDF | Print |

	Rebounds	Shots	FreeThrows	Fouls
	2	55		
	3	55	56	33
	4	55	25	
	44	55		
Totals	53	220	81	33

Chapter 6

Other Resources

We have looked at a great number of resources in this book, but of course there are always more. The mentioned Thesis theme and recommended plugins in this book are constantly updated on a regular basis, adding new features, improving existing capabilities, and hopefully becoming more secure. Be sure to visit your websites often to make sure they are all up to date. There will also be new plugins coming out all the time which may eclipse the plugins we recommended here. This chapter will help you go beyond this book and out into the wider WordPress community. The resources presented attempt to help you see just how vast the WordPress ecosystem really is and to give you the resources to help you locate answers to questions that have not yet been asked.

Online Resources

Starting with web resources we want to provide a list of websites where you can find answers you are seeking. We're going to go beyond the generic needle in the haystack process of using Google or Bing. We wanted to save you some time and therefore money by pointing you in the right direction.

Themes and Plugins

Naturally, since this book is about one major theme we want you to start your searching on the website hosting this theme, but we also know Thesis is not the be-all-and-end-all. There may be things you want to do that other themes will be better suited for. Of course, there is a seemingly endless list of themes on WordPress.org, but there are other places to find commercial (and therefore unfettered) themes. The very limited list is here:

- DIY Themes, *http://diythemes.com*
  Thesis Theme and supporting skins (and documentation)
- Build Your Own Business Website, *http://www.byobwebsite.com*
  Plugins and Skins for Thesis (free and commercial)
- WordPress Themes, *https://wordpress.org/themes/*
  Free themes and plugins
- Theme Forest, *http://themeforest.net*
  Commercial themes and plugins
- Creative Market, *https://creativemarket.com*
  Commercial themes and plugins
- iThemes, *https://ithemes.com*
  Commercial themes and plugins
- Tips and Tricks HQ, *https://www.tipsandtricks-hq.com*
  Commercial plugins
- Rocky Themes, *http://rockythemes.com*
  Commercial themes
- Creative Studio, *https://cr3ativ.com*
  Commercial themes and plugins

Written Materials

Of course, there are myriad of training and teaching materials on WordPress all over the internet. Blogs are what WordPress was invented for and reciprocally (ironically?) there are many blogs about WordPress. Below is a list of places with good training blogs, articles, courses, and books.

- WordPress News, *https://wordpress.org/news/*
  Latest news about WordPress releases and the community. Blog, support forum.
- Thesis from DIY Themes, *http://diythemes.com/thesis/*
  Blog from the makers of Thesis. Covers news, releases, ebooks, and has support forum for members.
- Build Your Own Business Website, *http://phpa.me/wp-byob-resources*
  Caters to helping small businesses develop, manage, and maintain a web presence with a blog, courses, seminars on Thesis, and support forum for members.
- Creative Market, *https://creativemarket.com/blog*

A platform for people to sell design assets including photos, graphics, templates, and themes. Provides free items each month.

- iThemes, *https://ithemes.com/blog/*
  WordPress News and updates. Includes posts about how to add different functionality to a blog and interviews with WordPress users.
- WP Tavern, *http://wptavern.com*
  A site focused on all things WordPress, but also covers any project from Automattic. Includes articles and podcasts, and is regularly updated.
- WP Squared, *http://www.wpsquared.com*
  Another useful blog. It also has guides ranging from how to disable comments to keeping your site secure. Offers theme and plugin reviews.
- WP Lift, *http://wplift.com*
  Founded to help by providing tutorials, news about WordPress, theme roundups, and plugin guides.

Conferences

One of the best ways to make contacts and get a more advanced education on WordPress topics at the same time is to attend conferences. Most of the WordPress related conferences are called WordCamps, but there are many other conferences which touch on WordPress and blogging in general. Also, there are advanced topics encompassing WordPress' foundation tools of PHP and MySQL. Here is a list of the conferences we know about, but no doubt there are many more. Visit WordCamp Central[1], to find a local WordCamp. WordPress is built with PHP, if you want to venture into programming your own themes and plugins, you can find a PHP conference near you on the PHP site[2]

[1]   *WordCamp Central: https://central.wordcamp.org*
[2]   *PHP Conferences: http://php.net/conferences*

Troubleshooting Assistance

If you need some detailed assistance with the WordPress core technology be sure to go to the documentation and the detailed *Codex* area, found at: *https://codex.wordpress.org* and looks like the image in Figure 6.1.

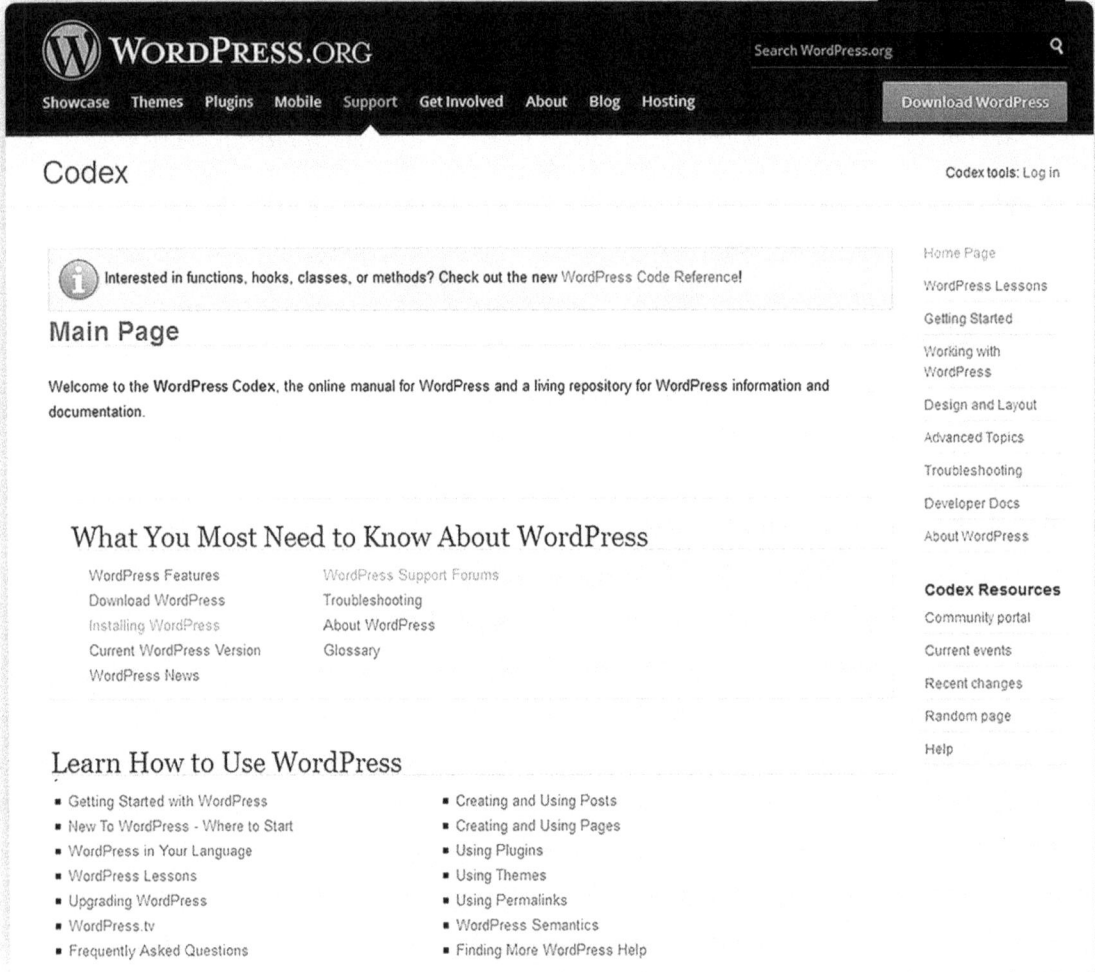

FIGURE 6.1

There are many pre-made links for you to explore. Note the list of additional Codex Resources on the right side bar as well. Each topic area has further sub-areas you can drill into for additional assistance on the issue at hand. For example, if you wanted to know about using plugins, you would read this article of information (Figure 6.2) after clicking on the top level link.

FIGURE 6.2

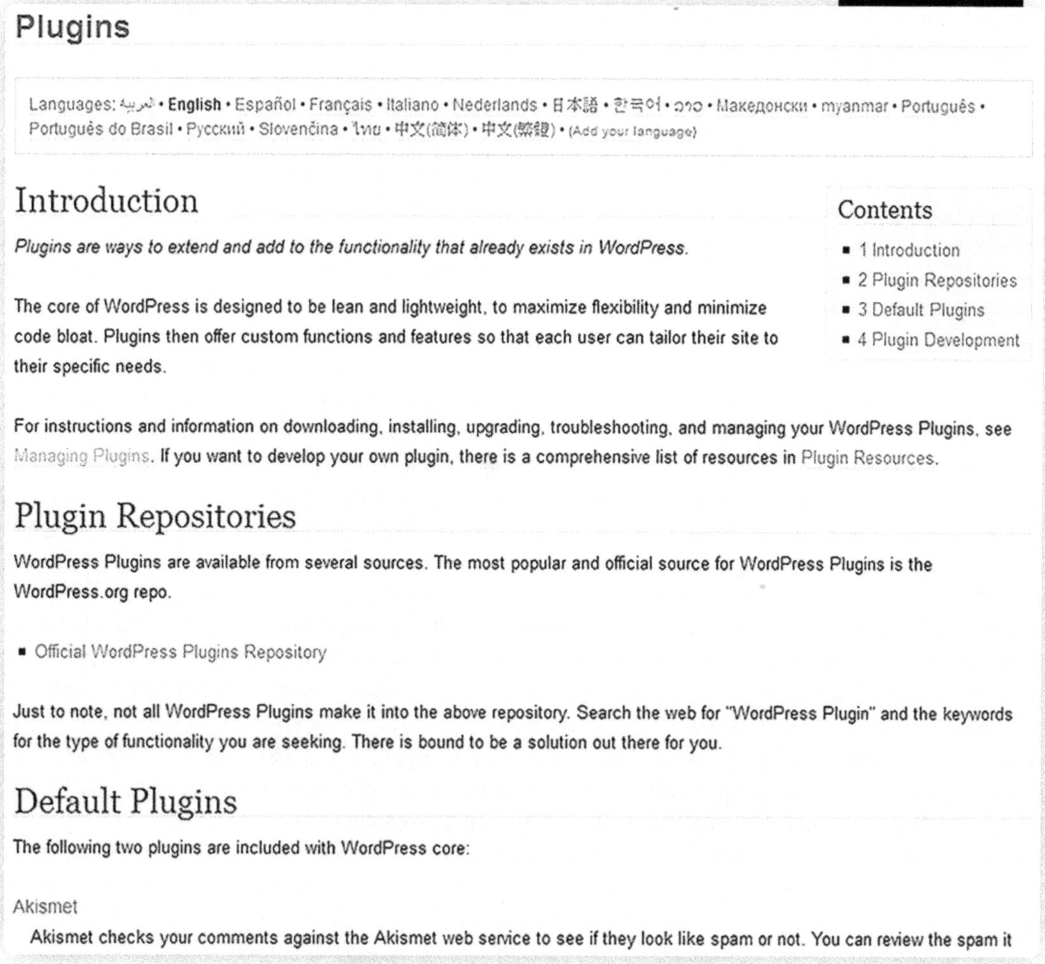

Plugins

Languages: العربية · **English** · Español · Français · Italiano · Nederlands · 日本語 · 한국어 · עברית · Македонски · myanmar · Português · Português do Brasil · Русский · Slovenčina · ไทย · 中文(简体) · 中文(繁體) · (Add your language)

Introduction

Plugins are ways to extend and add to the functionality that already exists in WordPress.

The core of WordPress is designed to be lean and lightweight, to maximize flexibility and minimize code bloat. Plugins then offer custom functions and features so that each user can tailor their site to their specific needs.

For instructions and information on downloading, installing, upgrading, troubleshooting, and managing your WordPress Plugins, see Managing Plugins. If you want to develop your own plugin, there is a comprehensive list of resources in Plugin Resources.

Contents

- 1 Introduction
- 2 Plugin Repositories
- 3 Default Plugins
- 4 Plugin Development

Plugin Repositories

WordPress Plugins are available from several sources. The most popular and official source for WordPress Plugins is the WordPress.org repo.

- Official WordPress Plugins Repository

Just to note, not all WordPress Plugins make it into the above repository. Search the web for "WordPress Plugin" and the keywords for the type of functionality you are seeking. There is bound to be a solution out there for you.

Default Plugins

The following two plugins are included with WordPress core:

Akismet

Akismet checks your comments against the Akismet web service to see if they look like spam or not. You can review the spam it

Now if all the above information somehow fails you, you can always go to the WordPress support forum[3] and ask your question. This is usually only done after you have exhausted the FAQ (Frequently Asked Questions) and the list of known issues. There is no need to ask the same question 50 times, to be certain, so spend some time trying to figure out your issue on your own first. There is no greater feeling of satisfaction than solving your own technical problems. Yet, if you have not found your answer then be sure to post the question on the forum here after you register and login as a member.

[3]   *WordPress support forum: https://wordpress.org/support/forum/how-to-and-troubleshooting*

Finding a Great Host

There is a certain skill in finding the perfect host from which to serve your great WordPress site(s). Without sharing my bias, once you find a host you are comfortable with, I highly recommended you stay with that host and not switch to another one at the first sign of trouble. These host companies want your business so they are motivated to quickly fix any issues which come up. See the guide at *https://make.wordpress.org/support/?p=41628* for advice on how to find a good hosting company. Keep in mind there are certain base levels of technology (PHP, MySQL, and a webserver like Apache) every WordPress site requires.

In particular, make sure your potential host is running a relatively recent version of PHP. Not only will you get better performance for your site, but older version of PHP are no longer supported. As I write this, PHP 5.5 is currently the oldest version that is receiving security and bug fixes from the core PHP team. Visit *http://php.net* to see the currently supported versions.

> NOTE: if you are building WordPress sites for clients as a business, then be sure to see if your potential hosting company has an affiliates program. This could give you a little extra cash for your hosting loyalty.

The Community

Lastly, we want to draw attention to the WordPress community. By this we mean the people and companies supporting the products that are out there. Keeping in mind all the resources listed earlier in this chapter, there are other places like social media where you can find people and companies talking about WordPress and related topics.

Here is a short list of Twitter users we are aware of that you should follow in the WordPress community. Of course there are many others and there are equally as many Facebook pages, but this should get you started. If you follow some or all of these accounts and then check out who they are following. You'll have more than enough connections to keep you current.

- *@WordPress*
- *@wordcamp*
- *@WCEurope*
- *@WordPressTV*
- *@Automattic*
- *@phparch*
- *@NEPHP*
- *@10up*
- *@nacin*
- *@EricMann*
- *@pbmacintyre*

Index

A

account
  administration, 4
  database user, 5
  developer, 93
admin, 10, 46
  area, 10, 12, 16, 36, 47, 66, 68
  dashboard, 54, 77
Akismet, 47–48
  menu option, 49
  plugin, 10, 44
  service, 48
analytics service, 40
Apache, 3, 112
API keys, 4, 48
Authorize Plugin, 77
Automattic, 109, 112
Autoupdate, 6

B

Backup Buddy, 54
backups, 33, 63–64, 100–101
  basic manual, 63
  saved, 101
Backup Scheduler, 100–101
Bing, 8, 107
blog post, single, 24
blog posts, 24, 28
Bluehost, 3, 5
Boxes, 15, 38, 61
Brute force attack protection, 74
bruteprotect.com, 9

C

caching, 104
Canvas, 30
Captcha, 98
Cart Pages, 92
codex.wordpress.org, 110
Commercial plugins, 90, 98, 108
Commercial themes, 11, 108
community, 45, 108, 112
conferences, 86, 109
Configuring Automatic Background Updates, 6
Contact Form, 41, 80–85
  DB, 80–81, 83–85
Copying Templates, 29
CSS, 1, 30–32, 34, 36, 62, 68, 89, 92, 101, 103, 105
  code, 35–36
  colors, 57
  editor, 30, 35
CSS Lint, 35
Custom CSS, 8, 34, 36
  editor, 34–35
customers, 91–93
  premium, 74–75
Custom Sidebars, 55
Custom Template area, 29

D

dashboard, 54, 98
database, 4–5, 35–36
Default Themes, 10, 13
development, 1–3, 63
  local, 3
development environments, 1, 3–4, 6, 16
Development Mode, 16, 37
devices, mobile, 69

DIY Themes, 15, 108
  website, 15

E

Easy Twitter Feed Widget, 71
eCommerce, 45, 55, 73
editing templates, 25
Editor CSS, 30
Email Broadcast, 98
Email Subscribers, 46–47, 49, 56
environments, 1–3
  deployed, 53
  designer, 22
  experimental, 2
  hosting, 4
  live, 73
export, 15, 33, 63, 84

F

Facebook, 40, 70, 98
favicon, 40
FileBrowser, 65
files, 2, 4–5, 32, 63, 65–66, 101
  basic install, 4
  configuration, 5
  copying, 101
  downloaded zip, 12, 16
  large, 67
  sm-template.php, 66
  wp-config.php, 6
financial integration, 93
firewall, 74
  rules, 75
Flickr, 70
font, 21, 42
form
  data, 81, 85
  designer, 82
Front Page, 23–24, 26, 61

FTP, 4–5, 45

G

GoDaddy, 3, 5
Google, 8–9, 15, 39–40, 76, 94, 102, 107
  account, 76–77
  Finance, 60
  fonts, 41
  Maps, 57
  spreadsheet, 101, 103, 105
Google+ information, 40
Google Analytics, 9, 39–40, 54, 73, 76
  account, 77
  Dashboard for WP, 9, 40, 76, 79
  information, 9, 76
  statistics, 9
  by Yoast, 76
Google Authorship and Site Verification, 40

H

Header Image, 21
Hexadecimal colors, 57
hosting platform, 3–4
HTML/Open boxes, 19

I

image
  gallery, 89
  slider, 86, 89
Inline Google Spreadsheet Viewer, 101, 103, 105
Instagram, 70
install
  plugins, 45
  WordPress, 3
Installing WordPress Locally, 3
iThemes, 108–9

L

Lamp, 3
layout, 13, 15, 19, 21, 24, 28, 34
  basic, 12, 81
  changes, 66
  default, 52
licenses, 15, 48
LinkedIn, 70
Linux, 3
login security, 74–75

M

MAMP, 3
Master Slider, 86–87
media library, 21, 32, 87
members, 2, 98–99, 108, 111
Membership Levels, 98–99
Meta Box, 96
MySQL, 2–3, 109, 112

O

online shop, 89, 91
Open Box, 38, 61
OpenHook, 39, 60–61
overlay, 18, 24, 26

P

page layouts, 15, 24
page templates, 15, 22–24, 91
passwords, 5, 9, 64, 75
  administration, 9
  strong, 75
PayPal, 89, 93, 99
PHP, 2–3, 5, 109, 112
  code, 26, 62–63
  Conferences, 109
  version of, 112
plugin installation, 46
popups, 68–69

Post Types, 95–96
Product Data, 90–91
production environments, 1–2
products, 6, 68, 89–91, 112

R

resources, 32, 36, 45, 107–8, 110, 112
responsiveness, 8
Responsive Touch Slider, 86
rotators, 51–53

S

Search Engine Optimization. See SEO
security, 6, 9–10, 112
  iThemes, 9
  vulnerabilities, 45
SEO, 8–9, 73, 94–95, 97
  content, 94–97
  meta tag content, 98
  plugin, 8, 97
SFTP, 4
sidebars, 19, 50, 53, 55–56, 60
Simple Links, 69
Simple Maintenance, 66
Simple Social Icons, 53
site
  tagline, 18, 25
  title, 25–26
Site Menu, internal Thesis, 40
Site Verification, 40
Skin Content, 17, 32, 62
Skin Design, 19–20, 32
skin editor, 15, 18–19, 22, 24–25, 27–31, 34–35, 39, 41, 61, 90–91
skins, 13, 15–23, 25, 27–28, 30, 33–38, 108
  active, 16, 18, 22, 30, 32–33, 37, 39
  changed, 32
  classic responsive, 13, 17, 36
  custom, 15

individual, 15

preview, 16, 37

slider, 86–89

images, 86, 88

Slider Controls, 89

slides, 86, 88–89

SL Plugins, 100

Snippet Preview, 96–97

Social Feeds, 70–71

social icons, 53

spam, 10, 47–49

SSL certificate, 93

staging, 1–2

Stock Keeping Unit, 90

Storefront, 90

Stripe, 93

subscribers, 51

SyncBack, 101

T

templates, 22–26, 28–29, 33, 36, 62–63, 87, 96, 109

custom, 24, 29, 33

design area, 27, 30

home, 26, 28–29

new, 29

pages, 24

Testimonial Rotator, 51

Thesis Skin Editor, 91

TinyMCE Color, 56

Tracking Scripts, 40

Troubleshooting Assistance, 110–11

Twitter, 40, 71, 98

Feed Widget, 70–71

Two-factor authentication, 75

U

Ubuntu, 3

Upload Theme, 12

User Experience, 58

W

WAMP, 3

Web server, 2, 41

website

analytics, 9

hosting, 47, 108

public, 27

Windows, 3

WooCommerce, 89–94

Thesis Integrator, 90

WordCamps, 109, 112

Wordfence, 6, 9, 74

Security, 74–75

WordPress

admin, 71

Codex, 3, 45

community, 107, 112

Install, 4–5

plugin, 9, 94

Popup, 68

support forum, 111

theme, 8, 11, 60, 108

WordPress environment, 3–4

WP Clone, 4, 63–64, 100

WP Currency Converter, 60

WP eMember, 98–99

Y

Yoast SEO, 94–95, 97

www.ingramcontent.com/pod-product-compliance
Lightning Source LLC
Chambersburg PA
CBHW062028210326
41519CB00060B/7204